The
Revolution
of 1911

By the Compilation Group
for the "History
of Modern China"
Series

FOREIGN LANGUAGES PRESS
PEKING 1976

Publisher's Note

The Revolution of 1911 is one of several booklets translated from the "History of Modern China" series, Shanghai People's Publishing House. Others are: *The Opium War* (1840-42), *The Taiping Revolution* (1851-64), *The Reform Movement of 1898* and *The Yi Ho Tuan Movement of 1900*. All were compiled by members of the history departments of Futan University and Shanghai Teachers' University. Some editorial changes have been made in the English version.

First edition 1976
Printed in the People's Republic of China

Sun Yat-sen, forerunner of China's
bourgeois-democratic   revolution.

檀香山興中會成立宣言

孫文

中國積弱，非一日矣！上則因循苟且，粉飾虛張，下則蒙昧無知，鮮能遠慮。近之辱國喪師，剝藩壓境，堂堂華下，不齒於鄰邦，文物冠裳，被輕於異族。有志之士，能無撫膺！夫以四百兆蒼生之眾，數萬里土地之饒，固可發奮爲雄，無敵於天下。乃以庸奴誤國，荼毒蒼生，一蹶不興，如斯之極。方今強鄰環列，虎視鷹瞵，久垂涎於中華五金之富，物產之饒，蠶食鯨吞，已效尤於接踵，瓜分豆剖，實堪虞於目前，有心人不禁大聲疾呼，亟拯斯民於水火，切扶大廈之將傾。用特集會衆以興中，協賢豪以共濟，抒此時艱，奠我中夏。仰諸同志，盍自勉旃，擬訂規條，臚列如左：

一、是會之設，專爲振興中華，維持國體起見。蓋我中華受外國欺凌，已非一日，皆由內外隔絕，上下之情罔通，國體抑損而不知，子民受制而無告。苦厄日深，爲害何極！茲特聯絡中外華人，創興是會以申民志，而扶國宗。

會中事務：

一、每逢禮拜四晚，本會集議一次，正副主席必要一位赴會，方能開議。

一、凡入會之人，每名捐會底銀五元。另有義捐，以助經費，隨人惟力是視，務宜踴躍赴義。

一、凡會中捐助各銀，皆爲幫助國家之用，必要由管庫存貯妥當，或貯銀行，以備有事調用。

一、本會公舉正副主席各一位，正副文案各一位，管庫一位，值理八位，差委二位，以專司理。惟管庫須有殷商二名擔保，以昭鄭重。

一、凡會中捐助各銀，皆爲幫助國家之用，除此不得動支，以省浮費。如或會中偶遇別事，要用小費者，可由會友集議妥允，然後支給。

一、凡新入會者，須要會友一位引薦擔保，方得准他入會。

一、凡會內所議各事，當照捨少從多之例而行，以昭公允。

一、凡以上所訂規條，會友須要恪守。倘有善法，亦可隨時當衆議訂加增，以臻完美。

Declaration of the Society for the
Revival of China at its founding, 1894.

Books and periodicals propagating revolution published before the Revolution of 1911.

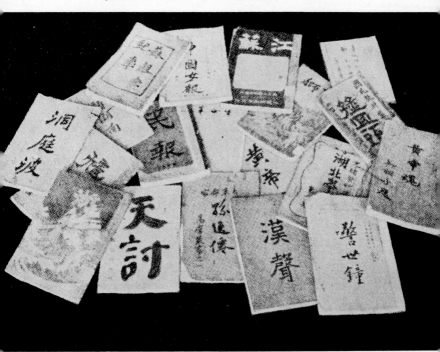

六之閣樓密秘事軍北湖

Secret command headquarters for the Wuchang
Uprising at No. 85, Hsiaochao Street, Wuchang.

The revolutionary army fights Ching Dynasty troops at Hankow.

Imperialist gunboats at Hankow in their attempted armed intervention against the Chinese revolution, October 1911.

United States forces of aggression landing in Shanghai to menace the revolution.

Ceremony inaugurating the Senate of the Provisional Government at Nanking, January 28, 1912 (Sun Yat-sen, fifth from left, front row).

Contents

Contents

Chinese Society Before the Revolution of 1911

At the end of the 19th and the beginning of the 20th century, world capitalism entered upon the stage of imperialism. The imperialist countries launched a series of aggressive wars for the seizure of colonies and also waged wars among themselves.

Subjected to aggression and oppression the people found life impossible and rose repeatedly in revolt. In this tempestuous era revolutionary flames spread throughout the world, and a period of critical upheavals began in China's modern history as well. Events of historical importance crowded this short space of less than two decades: the Sino-Japanese War of 1894; the Reform Movement of 1898; the Yi Ho Tuan Movement of 1900* and the invasion of China by the combined forces

---

* See *The Reform Movement of 1898* and *The Yi Ho Tuan Movement of 1900*, Foreign Languages Press, Peking, 1976.

of eight powers (Britain, the United States, Germany, France, Russia, Japan, Italy and Austria-Hungary) that same year; and finally the Revolution of 1911. All reflected the sharpening contradiction between the imperialist aggressors and the Chinese nation. The imperialists continued to expand their aggression against China and cruelly exploited the Chinese people; the Chinese people refused to submit and time and again launched large-scale movements of resistance. In this life-and-death struggle the reactionary Ching government daily revealed its odious features as a servile lackey of the imperialists.

After the invasion of China in 1900 by the allied forces of the eight imperialist powers, the traitorous Ching Dynasty government, headed by the Empress Dowager Tzu Hsi, proclaimed publicly that they hoped to "win the good graces of the powers, commensurately with China's resources." In other words, they would completely sell out the country and people to curry favour with the imperialists.

In the Ching government's bargain-sale of the country before the Revolution of 1911, tsarist Russia had seized a part of China's territory three times the size of France. Other imperialist countries had occupied China's Hongkong, Macao, Taiwan and the Penghu Islands, and forced the lease to them of

Kowloon, Kiaochow Bay, Lushun, Talien, Weihai-wei and Kwangchow Bay. These were grave encroachments on China's territorial integrity. The imperialists also forced China to open 82 of her coastal and inland ports to their trade and marked off areas in 16 cities as "concessions." In collaboration with the landlords, compradores and merchant-usury capital in many places, they set up a many-tiered structure of exploitation to fleece the Chinese people. Their investments in China mounted to 2,000 million silver dollars, more than 10 times those by China's national capitalists. They gained control over 80-90 per cent of China's heavy industry, communications and transport, and commodity markets. And through unequal treaties, loans and indemnities, they also seized control of China's customs and inland taxes. Thus they established domination over China's financial and economic lifelines. Their warships penetrated into China's territorial seas, inland waterways and lakes. Their armies of aggression had garrisons in China's big and medium cities and strategic points, even in the capital, Peking. There they set up their "legation quarter," really a super-government under which the corrupt Ching regime willingly played the role of "puppet emperor" as a tool of imperialist aggression. China retained independence only in name.

While the Ching government plunged deeper into treason in external affairs, it stepped up exploitation of the people within the country, all the more after signing the Protocol of 1901* with the imperialist aggressors. Before 1901 the Ching government's annual revenue averaged 80 million ounces of silver. It increased to 100 million in 1903, 230 million in 1908 and 300 million in 1910, almost quadrupling the burden of the people in less than 10 years. New taxes were piled on old under a variety of names, promoting corruption by provincial officials who increased taxes at every level until they were 10 or more times what the Ching government itself had authorized. Not only did exorbitant taxes and miscellaneous levies inflict ruin, break-up of families and homelessness upon the labouring masses; they also encroached on the interests of a section of the middle and small landlords. The reactionary, corrupt Ching regime thus

---

* After occupying Peking in August 1900 the eight-power allied army compelled the Ching government on September 7 of that year, to sign the traitorous Protocol of 1901. Under its provisions, China had to pay indemnities, dismantle her northern coastal forts and permit the stationing of foreign troops in Peking and 11 other strategic points, and the Ching government undertook to suppress all anti-imperialist organizations of the people. The Protocol of 1901 aggravated imperialist domination of China and proved that the Ching government had become an out-and-out tool of imperialist rule.

isolated itself as never before, and the contradiction between it and the people came to a sharp edge.

The Ching government, continuously selling out the country's sovereignty, paid most of the money it got from the people to the imperialists in indemnities and to defray the principal and interest of foreign loans. So the contradiction between the people and the Ching government became the focus of the contradiction between imperialism and the Chinese nation, as well as of that between feudalism and the great masses of the people. The Chinese people's great leader Chairman Mao Tsetung has pointed out: **"The Revolution of 1911 was directed against imperialism. The Chinese directed the revolution against the Ching regime because it was the running dog of imperialism."**

The labouring masses, the most cruelly exploited and oppressed by the Ching government, were the first to rise in revolt. Before the fire of the Yi Ho Tuan's* resistance to imperialist invasion in 1900-1901 had died down, the people in many places again took up arms against Ching rule. From 1901 to 1910 nearly 1,000 spontaneous struggles flared up throughout the country, involving tens of mil-

---

* The Yi Ho Tuan Movement which took place in north China in 1900 was a vast, spontaneous movement of peasants and handicraftsmen who rose in armed struggle against the imperialists.

lions of people. They increased in number and scope each year with the deepening of the Ching government's oppression. More than 80 were recorded in 1905, 130 in 1909 and 280 in 1910. Obviously, by the eve of the Revolution of 1911, the Ching Dynasty had undermined the foundations of its own rule by its perverse policies and measures. Dr. Sun Yat-sen, pioneer of China's bourgeois-democratic revolution, compared the Ching government to a tottering building beyond anybody's power to prop up.

These mass struggles created favourable conditions for speedy success of the Revolution of 1911, headed by the bourgeoisie. But the Chinese national bourgeoisie, because of its flabbiness, was neither willing nor able to lead the revolution to complete victory. In his "On New Democracy" Chairman Mao wrote of the characteristics of this class: **"Even when it takes part in the revolution, it is unwilling to break with imperialism completely and, moreover, it is closely associated with the exploitation of the rural areas through land rent; thus it is neither willing nor able to overthrow imperialism, and much less the feudal forces, in a thorough way. So neither of the two basic problems or tasks of China's bourgeois-democratic revolution can be solved or accomplished by the national bourgeoisie."**

6

The flabbiness of the Chinese national bourgeoisie (its vacillation and proneness to compromise) was determined by its economic position. Before the Revolution of 1911 the proportion of national-capitalist industries in the country's economy was low and their influence weak. In the 40 years from the 1870s to 1911, national capital had established only 500 modern factories with a total investment of 140-150 million silver dollars. This flimsy amount was less than half of the capital of old feudal-type Chinese pawnshops and money houses, to say nothing of ability to compete with imperialist investments in China. Under such circumstances, not only did the national bourgeoisie lack strength to resist foreign capital; it had to depend upon the imperialist countries for machinery and technological data. Some national industries went so far as to seek participation by foreign capital so as to secure protection and opportunities of growth under the signboard of a "Sino-foreign joint enterprise." Moreover, the national bourgeoisie had innumerable links with the feudal landlord class. Many of them came from landlord or official families which owned much land in the countryside and continued to practise exploitation through feudal land rent. Some had climbed up to be big bourgeois through their political positions in feudal society, which enabled them to secure privileges from the Ching government. This state of things determined their close ties with imperialism and feudalism.

Of course, the national bourgeoisie was a class with a dual character. It also had serious contradictions with imperialism and feudalism. In striving for self-enrichment and expansion, it ran smack up against the competition of foreign imports and suffered the blows of foreign capital. The traitorous Ching government facilitated the flooding of the domestic market by foreign goods while heavily taxing the products of national capitalist industry and restricting it in many ways. This further impaired the national bourgeoisie's ability to compete, and forced it, for the sake of its own development, to oppose imperialism and make the traitorous Ching government its immediate target of attack. The contradiction between the national bourgeoisie and the Ching government was determined by the semi-colonial and semi-feudal character of China at the time.

On the one hand, the national bourgeoisie was able to participate in the revolution. On the other, it was prone to compromise with the enemy. Its attitude towards the masses was also twofold — it could ally itself with the workers and peasants against the enemy, but also to ally itself with the enemy against the workers and peasants. This dual character of the national bourgeoisie was distinctly reflected in the whole process of the Revolution of 1911. Hence, this revolution could succeed to a certain degree, but was bound to fail in the end. The decisive factor was attitude towards the masses.

Chairman Mao says: **"Strictly speaking, China's bourgeois-democratic revolution against imperialism and feudalism was begun by Dr. Sun Yat-sen."** The founding of the revolutionary group known as the Hsing Chung Hui (Society for the Revival of China) marked the beginning of Sun Yat-sen's revolutionary activity.

Sun Yat-sen (Sun Wen) was born in 1866, in Tsuiheng Village, Hsiangshan (now renamed Chungshan) County, Kwangtung Province. The name Sun Chung-shan, by which he is best known in China, was one he later took while engaged in revolutionary activities in Japan, where he used the Japanese pronunciation of the last two characters — Nakayama.

An elder brother of his, Sun Mei, was an overseas Chinese capitalist in Honolulu, and Sun Yat-sen, at the age of 13, went to that city to live with him. There he attended missionary schools sponsored by British and American imperialists. In 1883 he returned to China, continuing his studies in Canton and in Hongkong, where he graduated in medicine at the Alice Memorial Hospital in 1892.

Thus Sun Yat-sen's education between 1879 and 1892 was entirely a Western bourgeois one, including many years in missionary schools. In those 13 years he learned natural science and also came in touch with the political theories of capitalist society, which played a considerable part in the formation of his ideology of bourgeois-democratic revolution.

While studying in Honolulu, Sun Yat-sen was inspired by the struggle of the Hawaiian people against U.S. aggression. He returned there in 1884 when U.S. imperialism was trying to annex the Hawaiian islands by every foul means. The heroic struggle of the Hawaiian people against foreign aggression indelibly impressed his young mind. Returning to China soon after, he was deeply shocked by the traitorous peace treaty signed with the French aggressors by the enemy of the people Li Hung-chang. The Sino-French War (1884-85) was a just one in which the peoples of China and Viet Nam together resisted the French invasion of the two countries, voluntarily joining each other in the battle and hitting the French invaders hard wherever they appeared. The new upsurge of national consciousness created a very favourable situation for victory over France. But this war ended in a humiliating treaty. Why? Thinking it over, Sun Yat-sen found the reason in the incompetence and corruption of the Ching government and its traitorous policy of fawning on foreigners. He became deeply dissatisfied with this government.

After qualifying as a physician in 1892, Sun Yat-sen practised in Macao and Canton. His concern with the destiny of the nation and country grew with each day, and he thought ceaselessly of how to struggle politically against Ching rule.

In 1894, returning to his home village of Tsuiheng Sun Yat-sen sent a "Petition to Li Hungchang," the powerful bureaucrat who then wielded major authority in the Ching government. It comprised a systematic political programme.

Sun's petition put forward the reformist political views he then held, which he summarized in four sentences: "Give the utmost play to people's abilities, develop the land to its utmost capacity, put materials to the utmost use, develop the flow of commodities to the utmost." Sun Yat-sen wanted the Ching government to follow the system of the Western bourgeoisie. Specifically he urged it to open schools for training various types of personnel; appoint officials responsible for agricultural administration and the development of irrigation so as to increase farm production; build mines, railways and factories and bring modern machinery into use; institute policies for the protection of trade, and enable the businessmen to make profits so they would exert themselves in enterprises. Plainly, he then took the stand of the bourgeoisie and hoped that, through a high feudal bureaucrat like Li Hung-chang, some social reforms favouring the development of capitalism might be made.

After sending his petition, Sun Yat-sen went to Shanghai and Tientsin to try to see Li Hung-chang in person. Li, a feudal bureaucrat subservient to foreign interests, had set up some industrial enterprises, both military and civilian, with machinery bought at high prices from Western capitalist countries. But his aim was to consolidate feudal-landlord rule, not develop capitalism. So he showed no interest in Sun Yat-sen's proposals and refused even to receive him. Thus Sun was rebuffed and his petition consigned to oblivion.

Following this failure, Sun Yat-sen went to Peking to find out what the Ching government really was and stood for. The time was at the outbreak of the Sino-Japanese War of 1894. The tragic defeat of the Chinese troops in the Asan campaign in Korea had shocked the whole nation, but the Ching rulers busied themselves, amid ceremonial songs and dances, with building the Summer Palace to celebrate the 60th birthday of the Empress Dowager Tzu Hsi. "A fall into the pit, a gain in one's wit," says the proverb. Through this experience, Sun Yat-sen saw for himself that political reform from above was impossible. Reformism was a blind alley. The only way was to overthrow the Ching government by violence. From then on, he became ever more eager for revolution. He went south to Wuhan to observe the situation in the Yangtze valley, then to Shanghai and finally to Honolulu to collect funds and assemble revolutionary forces in preparation for an armed uprising.

In Honolulu, Sun Yat-sen engaged actively in anti-Ching revolutionary propaganda among the overseas Chinese and won the support of the progressive section. In November 1894 he set up there the Hsing Chung Hui, China's first bourgeois revolutionary organization. It began with only 20 or so members, and later grew to 120.

In 1895, the Sino-Japanese War ended with China's defeat. The traitor Li Hung-chang, representing the Ching government, signed the Treaty of Shimonoseki, which cost China dear in sovereign rights and territory and aroused nation-wide indignation. Sun Yat-sen grasped the opportunity for action. He returned from Honolulu to Hongkong, organized the Hongkong Hsing Chung Hui and resolved on an armed uprising to seize Canton as a base for the revolution. The declarations made by the Hsing Chung Hui in Hongkong and Honolulu were similar in general principle, that is, they called for the revival of China and saving her from crisis, but the aim of the struggle was not made too clear. The membership oath of the Hongkong organization, however, stated: "Drive out the Tartars (the Ching imperial clan), revive the Chinese nation and establish a federal government." These points represented Sun Yat-sen's early revolutionary programme. They were initial expressions of his Principle of Nationalism and Principle of Democracy.

The Chien Heng Company in Hongkong, ostensibly a commercial firm, was in fact the legal cover of the Hongkong Hsing Chung Hui. It served as the headquarters for the Canton uprising. Some months later, Sun Yat-sen set up the Nung Hsueh Hui (Agricultural Society) in Canton itself. While appearing to be busy with the practice of medicine and promotion of farming, he carried on revolutionary activity among government officials, students and teachers, the Ching army, the

"Greenwood" groups* and secret societies. After half a year, this organization was able to rally nearly 10,000 persons. Making use of the local custom of visiting ancestral graves on the Double-Ninth Festival (ninth day of the ninth moon in the lunar calendar), Sun Yat-sen ordered all the forces of the uprising to gather at designated places in the guise of grave-visitors. He also commanded 3,000 members of these forces from Hongkong to take ship by night, with weapons and ammunition, to arrive at Canton on the festival morning. They were ordered to begin the attack on Canton as soon as the forces coming from different directions had made a junction. But when everything else was set, the Hongkong contingent failed to appear. At eight in the morning Sun Yat-sen received a telegram from Yang Chu-yun, who was in charge, saying it could arrive only two days later. Actually Yang, contending with Sun Yat-sen for leadership, had arbitrarily changed the plan and plunged things into confusion. All Sun could do was to disperse the gathering forces and telegraph the Hongkong contingent not to come. The next day the viceroy of Kwangtung and Kwangsi provinces, receiving information from a

* The "Greenwood" groups were armed bodies of peasants who gathered in the mountains and forests to fight feudal rule and eliminate local despotic landlords.

traitor within the Hsing Chung Hui, arrested Lu Hao-tung and other revolutionaries. Moreover, when Yang received Sun Yat-sen's telegram in Hongkong, a 200-strong force had already sailed, of whom more than 40 were arrested on landing at Canton. Though this uprising was suppressed before it could be launched it is historically significant as the overture to the Revolution of 1911.

After this failure, the Ching government issued many warrants, with promises of rewards, for the arrest of the revolutionaries. Sun Yat-sen, Chen Shao-pai and other leaders of the uprising escaped to Japan where they set up a Hsing Chung Hui branch in Yokohama. Leaving Chen Shao-pai in that city, Sun himself went on to Honolulu, the United States and England for revolutionary propaganda among overseas Chinese. He got to England in October 1896, and returned to Japan in July 1897 to make further plans for the Chinese revolution.

Sun Yat-sen's visit to Europe, though short, deeply influenced his thinking. He studied the literature of the revolutionary periods in capitalist countries in Europe and America, and investigated their current social and political conditions. Observation and research convinced him that the social system of capitalist countries was far from perfect. Political power was in the hands of the

17

wealthy few; and the disparities between the rich and poor led to constant social unrest and upheavals. Sun Yat-sen had the illusion that this malignant growth of capitalism could be avoided by building a flourishing oasis in the decaying capitalist world, thus preventing the future overthrow of the capitalist system in his idealized conception. The political ideas of social reform he later stood for, such as "equalization of landownership" and "regulation of capital," were intended to make up for the shortcomings of capitalism.

In June 1900, the Yi Ho Tuan Movement was in full swing in north China and the armed intervention by the allied forces of the eight imperialist powers began. Sun Yat-sen thought this was the time for an armed uprising, and went with a group of Hsing Chung Hui members to make preparations in Hongkong. But the British colonial authorities there would not let them land, so Sun Yat-sen had to call a conference on board ship. It was decided to launch the uprising in Sanchoutien in Huichow Sub-prefecture, Kwangtung Province. The main force was to consist of the "Greenwood" groups of Hsinan County and the San Ho Hui (Triad Society) members of Chiaying Subprefecture in the same province, using weapons borrowed from the Philippine independence fighters, who had originally bought them in Japan.

Afterwards, a drive would be made eastward along the coast to Amoy in Fukien Province. Sun Yat-sen reported that he had made an agreement with the Japanese governor of Taiwan that, when these forces reached Amoy, the Japanese government would support them with military supplies. At that point, Sun Yat-sen himself was to come over from Taiwan to personally command the insurgent forces equipped with Japanese arms. An attack on Canton would follow and, if it succeeded, a provisional government would be organized there.

In October Cheng Shih-liang, a member of the Hsing Chung Hui, was instructed by Sun Yat-sen to lead 600 San Ho Hui members in an uprising in Sanchoutien. They inflicted several defeats on the attacking Ching government troops and, within a fortnight, grew in number to more than 20,000. In the face of such strength, the Ching army could do nothing. When Sun Yat-sen in Taiwan got news of their successes, he telegraphed the Japanese Toruzo Miyazaki to send the arms borrowed from the Philippine independence fighters to Huichow. But those weapons turned out to be useless junk. And at this crucial moment, the Japanese government slapped a ban on the activities of Chinese revolutionaries in Taiwan and on supplying arms to them. Rendered helpless, Sun Yat-sen could do nothing more than inform Cheng

Shih-liang of the situation. The insurgent forces, whose morale had been high throughout half a month of sanguinary battles with the Ching army, used up their ammunition. When the eagerly awaited replenishment failed to arrive, they lost heart and their force of 20,000 men quickly disintegrated. Cheng Shih-liang, with some of his men, fled back to Hongkong.

Before the Huichow Uprising, Sun Yat-sen had sent Shih Chien-ju to Canton to seek support, but without success. Shih then resolved to assassinate Tehshou, Viceroy of Kwangtung and Kwangsi provinces. The explosives he used were too weak, and he was arrested and killed.

The failure of this second uprising was inevitable because Sun Yat-sen had led its participants into placing their hopes on Japanese imperialist support, neglected to co-ordinate their activity with other insurgent masses, and, most of all, because he had not gone among the masses to rally their support.

The continuously developing revolutionary situation after the Huichow Uprising encouraged Sun Yat-sen. He recalled later that following the abortive Canton Uprising in 1895 public opinion had branded him a rebel, outlaw and "heretic," but after the Huichow Uprising there was a big change, and many people sympathized with him over its failure. His remark vividly reflects the changing trend, with bourgeois-revolutionary activities not only attracting more and more attention but mounting to a tide that won ever greater public support. Hence, after the founding of the Hsing Chung Hui, many other bourgeois and petty-bourgeois revolutionary groups appeared. Two relatively prominent ones were the Kuang Fu Hui (Society for the Restoration of China) and Hua Hsing Hui (Society for the Revival of the Chinese

21

Nation). The former was an outgrowth of the Chun Kuo Min Chiao Yu Hui (Society for Military Education) set up by the Chinese students in Japan in 1903.

China's defeat in the Sino-Japanese War in 1895 proclaimed the bankruptcy of the "Westernization" or "learn from foreigners" movement.* What followed was the rise of the bourgeois reformism. Then the failure of the 1898 Reform Movement,** in its turn, proved reformism a blind alley. Afterwards many patriotic young people went abroad to study in search of a way to save the country and the people. Japan had succeeded in learning from the West. She was geographically nearer to China than the West, and less expensive for Chinese students. In the opening years of the 20th century their number there jumped from several hundred to 8,000. In Japan these young intellectuals came into contact with bourgeois

---

*From the 1860s to the 1890s, a section of the Ching government ruling group, more or less compradore in character, put Western capitalist technology to use to build factories, railways and mines. They dreamed of attaining "wealth and power" through such efforts, and thus maintaining their feudal rule. This was commonly called the "Westernization" or "learn from foreigners" movement.

** This movement was represented by persons like Kang Yu-wei, Liang Chi-chao, Tan Ssu-tung, Yen Fu and others. (For details, see *The Reform Movement of 1898*, Foreign Languages Press, Peking, 1976.)

ideology and culture. Most of them were dissatisfied with the imperialist tyranny over China and the incompetence and corruption of the traitorous Ching government, so they became sympathetic towards the daily broadening bourgeois-democratic revolution in the home country.

In 1900 when the allied army of the eight imperialist powers occupied Peking, tsarist Russia seized the opportunity to invade and occupy China's three northeastern provinces. At the beginning of 1903, in disregard of a previous agreement, she refused to withdraw her troops. Instead, she compelled the Ching government to sign a new agreement, attempting to legalize and perpetuate her occupation. This angered the entire Chinese people and a resist-Russia movement began. The people in the occupied Northeast resisted the Russian invaders with arms. Those in other provinces denounced the criminal aggression of Russian imperialism. In Peking, students of the Metropolitan College held rallies and signed petitions urging the Ching government to send troops against the invaders. In Shanghai, patriotic intellectuals headed by Tsai Yuan-pei called upon the people of the whole country to resist Russia in a circular telegram. Chinese students in Japan held a meeting and sent representatives with a petition demanding that the Ching government fight back with armed force. They also organized Resist-Russia Volunteers for military training preparatory to going to northeastern provinces to fight the Russian invaders. When the Japanese government banned their activities on the pretext of prohibiting military training by foreigners in Japan, the Resist-Russia Volunteers reorganized themselves into the Chun Kuo Min Chiao Yu Hui, which secretly sent people back to China to prepare armed revolution.

Before the founding of this organization two intellectuals in Shanghai, Tsai Yuan-pei and Chang Tai-yen, initiated the Chung Kuo Chiao Yu Hui (Educational Society of China) with Tsai as chairman. They carried out revolutionary propaganda in the guise of education, collected funds and planned to set up their own college. Students in Nanyang College in Shanghai were then on strike against the college authorities for suppressing their freedom of speech. More than 100 students had angrily left, so the Chung Kuo Chiao Yu Hui set up the Ai Kuo Hsueh Sheh (Patriotic Academic Society) for them. Later the students in the Army College at Nanking went on strike, and some came to Shanghai to join the society, considerably raising its prestige. The Chang Garden in Shanghai was a frequent venue of their speeches and other activities.

In the winter of 1903, students from Chekiang Province studying in Japan, who had been members of the Chun Kuo Min Chiao Yu Hui, cooperated with Tsai Yuan-pei and others to set up the Kuang Fu Hui in Shanghai under Tsai's chairmanship. Through one of its members, Tao Cheng-chang, this body made contact with secret societies in Kiangsu and Chekiang. Its line of resistance against the Ching government then became more clear-cut. It was a step forward from the Chun Kuo Min Chiao Yu Hui. In 1904, to further organize and develop the secret society forces, Tao Cheng-chang and others established contact with the Lung Hua Hui (Dragon Flower Society) and other organizations in Chekiang. The "Regulations of the Lung Hua Hui" included the slogan: "Transfer all land to public ownership and stop its usurpation by wealthy, despotic landlords." This slogan was welcomed by the members of the secret societies in Kiangsu, Chekiang and Anhwei. The Lung Hua Hui grew rapidly to fairly large size in the lower Yangtze valley.

While the Kuang Fu Hui was being founded in Shanghai three students from Hunan Province, Huang Hsing, Yang Tu-sheng and Chen Tien-hua, came back home from Japan to join in revolutionary work. In early 1904, in Hunan, they set up the Hua Hsing Hui with several hundred members, and the Tung Chou Hui (Society of Opposing the Common Enemy), which was a liaison organization with the secret societies. Ma Fu-yi, a leader of secret societies in Hunan, who was said to be able to rally more than 100,000 men, agreed to come under Huang Hsing's command. Huang Hsing and the others planned to seize Hunan by relying on the secret societies, then call for uprisings in all China's provinces to overthrow the Ching regime at one blow. They made the following concrete plan: On the 70th birthday of the Empress Dowager Tzu Hsi on the 10th day of the 10th lunar month, they would plant powerful explosives under the kneeling mats in the Imperial Hall of the Longevity Palace in Changsha. Thus they would kill all the civil and military officials assembled in the provincial capital for the celebration. Then, after occupying Changsha, they would muster support from many other Hunan cities, such as Yuehchow, Changteh, Liuyang, Hengchow, and Paoching. The main force of the uprising in Changsha was to be the students of the Military Academy who would also make contacts among the Ching garrison there, while in other places the members of the Ko Lao Hui (Society of Brothers) would make up the main force. But 10 days before the set date the information leaked out. The Ching government arrested several members of the secret societies, who revealed the plan and the identity of the leaders. Huang Hsing fled to Shanghai and later to Japan.

Both the names and the principles of the three organizations — the Hsing Chung Hui, Kuang Fu Hui, and Hua Hsing Hui — expressed their common objective of opposing the Ching government and overthrowing it by armed revolt. Their areas of operation included Kwangtung, Hunan, Hupeh and other provinces of the lower Yangtze valley. These quickly became centres of bourgeois-democratic revolution. The reasons were that they were relatively advanced in industry and commerce, had frequent contacts with the outside world, sent many students to study abroad and were the scene of acute conflict between new and old ideas, besides which they afforded a base in their secret societies, long devoted to "opposing the Ching and restoring the Ming Dynasty."

With the successive emergence of bourgeois and petty-bourgeois revolutionary groups, many kinds of publications propagating bourgeois-national revolution ideas and democratic thinking appeared. They were an important means used by the bourgeois revolutionaries to create revolutionary opinion, and were a major aspect of their activity. Such work included:

27

1. Reprinting books exposing atrocities by the Ching nobles when they seized control of the country in the 17th century, such as *Ten Days in Yangchow* and *The Massacre in Chiating*, to stir revolutionary nationalism against the Ching Dynasty.

2. Publication in large numbers of works by bourgeois revolutionary intellectuals, to expose the current corruption of the Ching government and its obsequious treachery in the face of imperialist aggression. Among such works were *The Revolutionary Army* by Tsou Jung, *Alarm Bell* and *Awakening* by Chen Tien-hua, and *Kang Yu-wei's Theory of Revolution Refuted* by Chang Tai-yen.

3. Compilation and translation of works written in the capitalist West during its period of bourgeois revolution, to introduce bourgeois-democratic revolutionary ideas. The Hsing Chung Hui founded the *Chung Kuo Jih Pao* (*China Daily*) in Hongkong. Chinese students in Japan put out periodicals such as *Yu Hsueh Yi Pien* (*The Compilation of Translations by Students Abroad*), *Ta Lu* (*Mainland*), *Hu Pei Hsueh Sheng Chiai* (*Hupeh Students News*), *Chiang Su* (*Kiangsu*), *Hsin Hu Nan* (*New Hunan*), and *Che Chiang Chao* (*Chekiang Tide*).

Most influential were the writings of Chen Tien-hua, Tsou Jung and Chang Tai-yen. Chen Tien-hua, in his *Alarm Bell* and *Awakening*, hailed the greatness of the Chinese nation and scathingly denounced the traitorous Ching government and the imperialists for trampling upon the Chinese people. His articles, simple and popular in language and fresh and lively in style, appealed to the common man. He wrote: "If foreign soldiers come, we should be brave. Don't be afraid of them. Students, lay down your pens! Peasants, drop your ploughs! Shopkeepers, stop your trading! Craftsmen, down tools! Everyone, sharpen swords and load guns! Drink a pledge in blood! Raise the cry: Forward! Kill the foreign devils! Don't rest until you have wiped out all enemies!" He called for the expulsion of the foreign aggressors, and the destruction of the traitors and flunkeys who served them, to attain the revolutionary aims of "revision of treaties, recovery of lost sovereign rights and achievement of complete independence." These ideas were warmly acclaimed by the revolutionary people. Tsou Jung in *The Revolutionary Army* wrote with similar simplicity of language, wealth of feeling and boldness of thought. Mercilessly exposing and castigating Ching rulers' cruel oppression of the people, he propagated his political views: overthrow of the Ching regime, struggle against foreign intervention, equality for all the people and the establishment of a bourgeois republic. He called on the people to "assail the Aisin Gioros (surname of the Ching imperial clan) with a forest of spears and a hail of bullets," overthrow the Ching government, and then sweep out the "demons from abroad" who were infringing China's sovereignty.

All these books won immediate public attention. Chang Tai-yen, already a famous scholar, came out in open refutation of the reactionary monarchist ideas of Kang Yu-wei. The latter, at the time, was shamelessly lauding the "sacred virtue" of the Kuang Hsu Emperor and viciously slandering the revolution — exerting a sinister influence. Chang Tai-yen refuted him with force and thoroughness, and publicly called the Kuang Hsu Emperor an ignorant clown who could not even tell wheat from rice. In the feudal society in which the emperor was the supreme authority, such bold words naturally threw the Ching rulers into shock and confusion. Precisely for this reason, they were warmly received by the revolutionary people.

Faced with political and ideological attack by the revolutionaries, the Ching government resorted to high-handed suppression. In 1903, the *Su Pao (Kiangsu News)* incident had a nation-wide impact. The *Su Pao* was published in a foreign concession in Shanghai, originally by Chen Fan, a county magistrate who had lost his post. From a reformist he had turned towards revolution. The Chung Kuo Chiao Yu Hui and the Ai Kuo Hsueh Sheh made this paper an organ for their propaganda. When *The Revolutionary Army* was published in Shanghai, the *Su Pao* printed articles recommending and praising the pamphlet and also reproduced *Kang Yu-wei's Theory of Revolution Refuted* by Chang Tai-yen. The journal thus became a thorn in the side of the Ching rulers who, with the collaboration of the imperialists, closed it down and arrested both Chang Tai-yen and Tsou Jung. Tsou died in prison and Chang received a three-year sentence.

Though the Ching government banned many other revolutionary publications, its despicable attempts to crush revolutionary opinion were futile. After the closure of the *Su Pao,* the revolutionaries put out another and much bigger paper, the *Kuo Min Jih Jih Pao (Citizens' Daily).* The more the revolutionary publications were suppressed, the more people wanted to read them. Tsao Ah-kou, a peasant in Chekiang Province filled with the spirit of revolt, got a copy of *Awakening,* read it avidly and began to make speeches everywhere about revolution. The Ching government arrested and executed him. It proclaimed that all who read the rebel book *Awakening* would be summarily condemned to death. But afterwards even more people sought the book. Failing to get it in the countryside, they tried by different means to get it from Shanghai. The same kind of thing happened elsewhere. The revolutionary trend was irresistible. Reactionary efforts at prohibition and suppression only quickened the people's awakening. The proof was that, before the Revolution of 1911, revolutionary books and pamphlets spread everywhere, breaking through all barriers.

China's internal situation changed drastically in the 10 years between the establishment of the Hsing Chung Hui (Society for the Revival of China) in 1894 and the emergence of the Kuang Fu Hui (Society for the Restoration of China), the Hua Hsing Hui (Society for the Revival of the Chinese Nation) and other revolutionary organizations. After signing the Protocol of 1901, the Ching government had sold out completely to the foreign imperialists and the people of all China's nationalities were crying out for the overthrow of the traitor regime. The new situation required rapid formation of a unified revolutionary party to lead the bourgeois-democratic revolution on a nation-wide scale. The founding of the Tung Meng Hui (China Revolutionary League) answered to the objective situation. With it, China's bourgeois-

33

democratic revolution began to move towards its high tide.

While revolutionary organizations mushroomed within the country, revolutionary forces among the overseas Chinese also grew. In the winter of 1903, Sun Yat-sen arrived once more in Honolulu. Many of the overseas Chinese there were the members of the Hung Men (also known as Hung Pang, or Red Band, one of the secret societies of the Ching Dynasty period), so Sun, to facilitate his own activity, joined one of its constituent bodies, the Chih Kung Tang (Promote-Public-Interest Group). Early in 1904, in the capacity of a leader of this secret organization, he did revolutionary propaganda among the overseas Chinese in North America and was welcomed by them. He personally revised the statutes of the Chih Kung Tang there, inserting as their main principle the words of the oath of the Hsing Chung Hui with important changes so that it now read: "Drive out the Tartars, revive the Chinese nation, establish a republic and equalize landownership." Thenceforward, the important idea of "equalization of landownership" became part of the revolutionary programme of Sun Yat-sen. At the beginning of 1905, he left America for Europe to set up revolutionary organizations among Chinese students there.

The multiplication of revolutionary organizations in China and abroad reflected the constantly developing revolutionary situation. At the same time, it faced the revolutionaries with a new task — the merging of their numerous small groups into one unified party to lead the revolution forward. In July 1905, Sun Yat-sen went to Japan, where in the light of this objective necessity he consulted with Huang Hsing and Sung Chiao-jen, representatives of the Hua Hsing Hui, on appropriate action. Huang and the others were in favour. They concluded that a unified revolutionary party should be set up on the basis of the organizations of the Hsing Chung Hui and the Hua Hsing Hui, in association with the Kuang Fu Hui and other bodies.

On July 30, 1905, in Tokyo, the first joint meeting of more than 70 delegates from revolutionary organizations was held. It decided to establish the China Revolutionary League. As its political programme, it took Sun Yat-sen's slogan, consisting of 16 Chinese characters: "Drive out the Tartars, revive the Chinese nation, establish a republic and equalize landownership."

On August 13, the Chinese students in Japan held a meeting in Tokyo to welcome Sun Yat-sen. More than 1,300 attended — the hall overflowed, some people even stood in the doorsteps — an unprecedentedly impressive gathering. Sun Yat-sen in his speech called for action, sharply refuting the fallacy of the reformists that "China can adopt only a constitutional monarchy, not a democratic republic." His address heightened the determination of the revolutionaries to fight — it unfurled the revolutionary banner. On August 20, the inaugural session of the China Revolutionary League, with several hundred members attending, met in Tokyo. It adopted the programme of the League and the "Manifesto of the Military Government" (also known as the "Manifesto of the China Revolutionary League"), and elected Sun Yat-sen *tsungli* (director-general). Under this programme, the League set up its headquarters in Tokyo. It had three departments — executive, consultative and judicial. Huang Hsing headed the general affairs office of the executive department, and carried on the headquarters' routine for Sun Yat-sen.

In November, this headquarters began publication of the *Min Pao* (*People's Journal*), organ of the League. In introductory remarks to the first issue Sun Yat-sen elaborated his 16-character programme as consisting of three principles — nationalism, democracy and people's livelihood. These were the old Three People's Principles advanced in the period of the bourgeois-democratic revolution. In them, "nationalism" referred mainly to "driving out the Tartars and reviving the Chinese nation," "democracy" mainly to "the establishment of a republic," and "people's livelihood" mainly to "the equalization of landownership." These four phrases (the 16 characters) and three principles made up the basic content of Sun Yat-sen's social and political ideology. They were the guiding ideas with which he would lead the Revolution of 1911.

Subsequently, the headquarters of the League formulated its "Programme for Revolution." It consisted of eight documents, including the "Manifesto of the Military Government" and "Manifesto to the World" and embracing its policies for general administration, for foreign affairs and specifically for armed uprisings in the various parts of the country.

The founding of the League marked a big step forward in China's bourgeois-democratic revolution.

First, the recognition of Sun Yat-sen's Three People's Principles as the guiding thought of the League indicated that the bourgeois revolution had reached a higher degree of maturity.

In expounding nationalism Sun Yat-sen abandoned the idea of national revenge in the old slogan of opposition to the Manchus. "Nationalism does not mean discriminating against nationalities other than the Hans," he said. "We do not hate all Manchus but only those who have harmed the Han people. We have no reason at all to wreak vengefully on any Manchus who do not hinder or harm the coming revolution." Although he still drew no distinction between the Manchu aristocrats and commoners, this interpretation of nationalism was an undoubted advance in outlook as compared with the concept of national revolution propagated by the anti-Manchu section of the landlord class.

Sun Yat-sen interpreted the Principle of Nationalism as one of struggle to seize power from the Ching Dynasty aristocrats. He said: "The overthrow of the Manchu government is a national revolution in the sense of driving out the Manchus, and also a political revolution in the sense of toppling the monarchy. But that is not to say it requires to be made two times. The political revolution will bring the establishment of a constitutional democracy. In our present political view, a revolution would be necessary even if the monarch were of Han nationality." Here Sun Yat-sen was combining the national revolution with the democratic revolution, laying the theoretical basis for the ensuing overthrow of the Ching government which would at the same time end the 2,000-year-old system of feudal monarchy in China.

Sun's Principle of People's Livelihood, though purely utopian, gave first importance to the equalization of landownership, which pointed to the essence of anti-feudalism.

Secondly, with the founding of the China Revolutionary League as one unified revolutionary party in place of the hitherto small and isolated groups, the revolutionaries became more united and stronger than ever before.

The previous revolutionary bodies — such as the Hsing Chung Hui, the Kuang Fu Hui and the Hua Hsing Hui — all bore deep marks of the old secret societies, and were rather local in scope. As a rule, they had neither regular political programmes nor integrated organizational form. Each went its own way and, even internally, lacked co-ordination. The establishment of the China Revolutionary League changed this.

Sun Yat-sen, and the Hsing Chung Hui founded by him, had long worked mainly in Kwangtung Province, Hongkong and among the overseas Chinese, with little contact with the people in inland provinces. The founding of the China Revolutionary League brought a great increase in membership and contacts within the country. Most of the new recruits were students who had returned to the provinces from schools abroad, and intellectuals associated with them. Most of them, though coming from landlord or bourgeois families, were petty-bourgeois in their actual social position. They had youth, enthusiasm, and were disgusted with the dark rule of the Ching government. So they were quite revolutionary, and their entry into the League gave it added strength.

Nonetheless, the League was no more than a loose alliance of the bourgeois and petty-bourgeois revolutionaries plus anti-Manchu elements from the landlord class. So, while on the surface it had accepted Sun Yat-sen's Three People's Principles as the ideological guide in its work, many members had reservations. Some of those originally in the Hua Hsing Hui and other organizations came from big-landlord families and in fact accepted Sun Yat-sen's ideas of nationalism and democracy but opposed the equalization of landownership — so they were dubbed "believers in two people's principles." Others, from the Kuang Fu Hui, emphasized the anti-Manchu struggle and neglected other aspects, and hence were nicknamed "believers in one people's principle." Political dissension in the League led to organizational instability. Before long, a body calling itself the Kung Chin Hui (Society for Mutual Progress) branched off from the League and, still in the latter's name, spread the ambiguous idea of "equalization of the human rights" in place of "equalization of landownership." The Kuang

Fu Hui, too, kept on flying its own colours and acting on its own. All this foreboded the future crisis of splits in the League.

A serious problem was the grave weaknesses in the League programme itself.

First, its Principle of Nationalism was directed exclusively against the regime headed by the Ching aristocracy and left out imperialism. Thus it neglected the principal contradiction of modern Chinese society — that between the imperialist aggressors and the Chinese nation. Although Sun Yat-sen, Chen Tien-hua and others held patriotic, anti-imperialist views, their bourgeois world outlook and political stand led inevitably to some illusions about imperialism. Hence they could not deeply understand the aggressive essence of imperialism, or transmute their patriotic, anti-imperialist ideas into a programme for concrete action. This was all the more true of League members with a deeply feudal tinge, who had never been happy about "the establishment of a republic and the equalization of landownership." Their propaganda constantly exaggerated the contradiction between the Manchu and Han nationalities, which was in fact only a secondary one, into the principal contradiction of modern Chinese society, thus greatly diluting the anti-imperialist content of the 1911 Revolution. The League's "Manifesto to the World" shows clearly that the Principle of Nationalism upheld by the bourgeois revolutionaries was still so narrow as to allow great illusions about imperialism.

The "Manifesto" was composed of seven articles. The first three were:

1. "All past treaties concluded by China with other countries will remain in force."
2. "All indemnities and foreign loans will continue to be paid."
3. "All privileges now enjoyed by foreigners will be protected."

This represented the League's general principle in foreign affairs. Obviously the "Manifesto" was issued to curry favour with the imperialists. It told them plainly that the bourgeois revolutionaries intended to recognize their privileges in China, that is, to accept China's semi-colonial position in exchange for support or neutrality by the imperialists. Yet the Ching government was a stooge of the imperialists and revolution against it meant anti-imperialist revolution. How could the imperialists support it, or stay neutral? So the bourgeois revolutionaries' lack of revolutionary thoroughness was revealed, first of all, in their political programme.

Secondly, although Sun Yat-sen explained the Principle of Nationalism as a struggle to seize power from the Ching aristocrats, his class limitations prevented his seeing that they were the political representatives of the landlord class. So some of his followers applied this principle simply as one of struggle against the Manchus — greatly weakening the anti-feudal significance of the 1911 Revolution. The League's "Call to the Manchu Officers and Soldiers for Surrender" showed how lacking in political content was the Principle of Democracy of the bourgeois revolutionaries, and the illusory hopes they placed on the bureaucrat-landlords and feudal warlords of Han nationality.

The "Call" began with an address to Han bureaucrats and warlords who had worked hard for the Ching government. Both the revolutionaries and they were Chinese, it declared. "In natural sentiment you are our brothers, in position you are our enemies." But it went on, both were oppressed by the Ching government; so once these bureaucrats and warlords stopped "suffering patiently without protest" and rose against the Ching government they would be "no longer our enemies but our brothers." Such tunes were more likely to spread illusions among the revolutionaries about the Han reactionaries than to win the latter over. Furthermore, the League's "Administrative Regulations for Taken-Over Areas" provided that, after the uprising, the maintenance of local social order would be entrusted to the local landlords and gentry. This demonstrated all the more clearly the bourgeois revolutionaries' proneness to compromise with the feudal landlord class.

Finally, although it had put forward the slogan "equalization of landownership" the League opposed the revolutionary action by the peasants to "turn land seized from the rich families into their own." They had vain imaginings about solving the land problem by the "land assessment" method. This called for the price of every piece of land to be fixed by the revolutionary government, with the fixed value remaining the property of the original landowner while all increases in the price of the land accruing from the social progress after the revolution would go to the state, or be "shared by the citizens" (which in practice would mean shared by the bourgeoisie with no share for the peasant masses). The scheme revealed fear of the peasants' rising to destroy by violence the foundation of feudal rule — ownership of land by the feudal landlord class. Hence it could not meet the peasants' urgent demand for land, or contribute to any great change in the countryside. Here was a clear indication that the Chinese bourgeoisie could not provide real leadership for the peasants, the main force of the democratic revolution, in the struggle against feudalism. This was the fatal weakness of the Chinese bourgeoisie.

Struggle Against the Reformists

After the establishment of the China Revolutionary League, as before it, the bourgeois reformists represented by Kang Yu-wei and Liang Chi-chao continued extremely active. Taking advantage of political influence gained in the previous period, they spread monarchist demagogy to mislead the people and emerged as implacable enemies of the revolution. To sweep away this obstacle and push the revolution forward, the bourgeois revolutionaries struggled against the reformists. Sun Yat-sen was the standard-bearer of China's revolutionary democrats in this struggle.

It took some time for the bourgeois revolutionaries to get to know what the reformists really were and stood for.

In November 1896 the reformists started the newspaper *Chih Hsin Pao* (*New Knowledge*) in

45

Macao. Some members of the Hsing Chung Hui (Society for the Revival of China) offered to co-operate with it but were rebuffed. In 1897 the overseas Chinese in Yokohama, Japan, planned to set up a school and asked Sun Yat-sen to find teachers in China. Chen Shao-pai, a Hsing Chung Hui member, told them to contact Liang Chi-chao in Shanghai. The reformists, then expanding their forces abroad, sent Kang Yu-wei's pupil Hsu Chin and others to Yokohama. Sun Yat-sen named the school "Chunghsi" (China-West). But Hsu Chin and his associates, after they arrived, changed it to "Tatung" (Great Harmony) at the instance of Kang.

In 1898 the Kuang Hsu Emperor accepted reform proposals by Kang Yu-wei and others and promulgated them in imperial edicts. Thinking that they had the upper hand, and fearing that their own ranks would be disrupted by the contacts of Hsu Chin and his associates with the revolutionaries in Japan, the reformists put up a poster in the Tatung School: "Don't receive Sun Yat-sen." Thereafter Sun Yat-sen was denied entry there. Thus this school, founded by the revolutionaries, was taken over by the reformists. It became the centre for their activities abroad.

In September 1898, the Empress Dowager Tzu Hsi launched a coup d'état, put the Kuang Hsu

Emperor under house arrest and had Tan Ssu-tung and some other reformists executed. Kang Yu-wei and Liang Chi-chao, protected by certain British and Japanese imperialists, fled to Japan. Sun Yat-sen wanted to take the opportunity to establish co-operation with the reformists, but a series of negotiations came to nothing. Under the shock of the coup d'état, the reformists were splitting up. Some tended towards revolution and joined the Hsing Chung Hui. Others like Kang Yu-wei and Liang Chi-chao stuck to their bankrupt reformism and turned into die-hard monarchists.

In 1899 Kang Yu-wei left Japan for Canada to sponsor the Pao Huang Hui (Protect-the-Emperor Society) there. Liang Chi-chao appeared in somewhat different guise in Japan, starting the newspaper *Ching Yi Pao (Honest Opinion)*. In it, on the one hand, he sang the praises of the Kuang Hsu Emperor and on the other hand, attacked the Empress Dowager and wrote articles against the Ching government, pretending to be very radical. In October that year, also in Japan, he opened the Tatung College where he taught students the Western bourgeois version of freedom, equality and natural human rights. Many people were hoodwinked by this. Even Sun Yat-sen believed that Liang had turned towards revolution and was prepared to form a political party jointly with him.

The reason Liang Chi-chao put on these revolutionary airs was that after the collapse of the Reform Movement of 1898 the situation changed. The bourgeois revolutionaries represented by Sun Yat-sen could straighten their backs. They established contact with secret societies within the country, and expanded the revolutionary forces in Honolulu and Japan. To make use of the position of the revolutionaries to pile up some strength for themselves, Liang Chi-chao and his ilk adopted the crooked tactics of putting on a revolutionary face while inwardly staying monarchist. The revolutionaries were not vigilant enough about this. In 1899 they introduced the leaders of some secret societies in the Yangtze valley to the monarchists. This enabled the latter, on their return home, quickly to win over these societies and establish a new organization headed by Kang Yu-wei with Liang Chi-chao as his deputy. In 1900, Sun Yat-sen himself introduced certain Hsing Chung Hui members in Honolulu, including his own brother Sun Mei, to Liang Chi-chao. As a result, when Liang came to Honolulu he used the names of Sun Yat-sen and his brother and, pretending to be "monarchist only superficially but revolutionary within," went all out to enlarge the Pao Huang Hui. Many Hsing Chung Hui members were pulled in and even Sun Yat-sen's brother became one of its leaders.

In 1903, Sun Yat-sen returned to Honolulu only to find the monarchist forces very strong. Realizing that he had been tricked by Liang Chi-chao, he began rectifying and strengthening the revolutionary organizations and wrote articles such as "To Our Fellow Countrymen" and "Refute the Monarchist Newspaper" to expose the deceptive propaganda of the monarchists. He also instructed the various Hsing Chung Hui branches to open newspapers and others to readjust their work so as to subject the monarchists to strong criticism. In Honolulu the *Min Sheng Jih Pao* (*People's Livelihood Daily*) took up the battle against the reformists' *Hsin Chung Kuo Pao* (*New China*), and in San Francisco the *Ta Tung Pao* (*Great Harmony*) opposed the *Wen Hsing Pao* (*Literary Revival*). In Canton, Shanghai, Tientsin and Hongkong, and in Singapore, Siam and Japan, revolutionary newspapers were started to criticize the reformists.

The founding of the China Revolutionary League in 1905 brought the revolutionaries' struggle against the reformists to high tide. The new-born League decided to make the paper *Erh Shih Shih Chi Chih Chih Na* (*Twentieth Century China*) run by Huang Hsing and others in Tokyo into its own organ and in September 1905, decided to rename it the Min Pao (People's Journal). Regular publication began in November.

The very first issue, in its opening article, proclaimed the battle against the reformists. Later, the paper propagated the ideas of the bourgeois-democratic revolution in the West. It also carried articles and reports about the Russian Revolution of 1905, lauding its participants' "unswerving and dauntless" revolutionary spirit, with which it wanted to infuse Chinese revolutionaries as well. Every issue of the Min Pao circulated widely among the progressive people of China and had to be reprinted again and again.

The reformists, who feared the overthrow of the Ching government, hated the upsurge of the bourgeois-democratic revolution. Liang Chi-chao explicitly stated their fear in a letter to Kang Yu-wei. "Today our deadly struggle against the government is of secondary importance to our party," he wrote, "while our deadly struggle against the revolution is of first importance. It is them or us. But if we don't fight things out with the government we have no hope of winning the country-wide support and eradicating the influence of the other party (meaning the revolutionaries). Therefore our fight against the government also brooks no delay." This showed the reformists' reactionary stand. It consisted of attacking the Ching government in a small way in words, aiding it in a big way in deeds, and trying to block the revolution while fooling the people. So a great debate between the revolutionaries and the reformists was inevitable.

In 1906, at the celebration of the *Min Pao*'s first anniversary, Chang Tai-yen gave a speech reiterating the principles of national revolution and establishment of a republic. Sun Yat-sen spoke on the political essence of the Three People's Principles. Both were violently attacked by Liang Chichao's *Hsin Min Tsung Pao (New People's Miscellany)* and the debate became fiercer.

The reformists cooked up many specious reasons for defending the Ching government, opposing the revolutionaries' advocacy of national and political revolution, and opposing revolutionary violence and the overthrow of Ching rule.

They argued that the Han people had already achieved complete equality with the Manchus, in legal status and political life, and a national revolution was therefore entirely unnecessary.

They pretended to have been for a political revolution all along, but said it should be carried out through "appropriate" principles, that is, by "advising" the government to reform its politics and "demanding" that it change to a constitutional monarchy.

They ranted that a "bad" people made for a bad government and without a "good" people politics would deteriorate still more if the government gave up its autocratic pressure. So, the trouble was not that the government was bad but that the people were bad.

They clamoured that political reforms "could only be carried out step by step," and "not a single step must be skipped." They even talked such nonsense as that the Chinese people were unqualified for citizenship in a republic for lack of ability to operate a democratic political system. Hence, they said, the only thing possible was for an enlightened absolutism to first educate the people in "concern for public interest" and "self-government," after which the emperor could graciously grant a constitutional monarchy.

They preached cravenly to the revolutionaries that stubborn insistence on armed revolution and a democratic political system in China would inevitably bring riot and revolt by "people of the lower strata," undermining social order and leading to intervention by the imperialist powers, placing the country in danger of partition and extinction.

The revolutionaries refuted these barefaced rumours and sophistries. Citing a wealth of facts, they proved that the Ching government consistently practised the reactionary policies of national discrimination and oppression. Its rule had made China a prison of nationalities, and was an obstacle to democracy. Hence both national and political revolution was absolutely necessary.

The revolutionaries ripped off the reformists' mask of "political revolution." They branded the "appropriate" principles spoken of by the reformists as simply apologetics for the Ching government, advanced from a reactionary stand to oppose revolution. They cited the history of revolutions in European capitalist countries to prove that without revolution by violence, without employing armed force, even a constitutional monarchy was impossible. The reformist homilies about achieving an "enlightened absolutism" and "constitutional monarchy" by kowtowing and petitioning were sheer fraud. Their real purpose was to consolidate the "barbarous autocracy" of the Ching government.

The revolutionaries were confident that China, though a late-comer in modern development, could catch up with it, and in a few years "not only surpass Japan," but "possibly have all that Western civilization already has," and sharply repudiated the reformists' reactionary fallacy that "not a single step must be skipped." Basing themselves on the bourgeois theory of "natural human rights,"

53

they also refuted the reformist myth that "the people were bad." Provided the autocratic monarchy was shaken off, they contended, the people would surely go into action of their own accord and struggle for democratic rights. Citing the failure of the Reform Movement of 1898 as an example, they proved that the Ching government, though already rotten to the core, would not relinquish a single crumb of its power. The reformists were exerting themselves to apologize for such a decadent and stubborn government and to cajole it into establishing a constitutional monarchy. Nothing could more effectively prove that the reformists and the Ching government were jackals from the same lair.

The revolutionaries, therefore, openly hoisted the banner of armed revolution and called for forcible overthrow of the Ching government. They pointed out that it had long become a servile tool and stooge of imperialism. To save the country from partition and extinction, this government of national betrayal had to be knocked down. But the reformists were still trying to preserve the Ching rule by every means, so their vaunted "love of country" was in fact just "love for the Ching government." Both it and they were traitors, selling out the country and people.

This debate lasted for many years with the revolutionaries winning ever higher prestige and the reformists falling into ever deeper disrepute. In 1907 Liang Chi-chao organized in Japan the Cheng Wen Sheh (Political Information Association), as a prop for the sham constitutional monarchy the Ching government was finally rigging up. More than 1,000 people attended the inaugural ceremony, but among them only some 200 were reformists, while 1,000 were revolutionaries or persons inclined towards the revolution. So as soon as Liang Chi-chao stepped onto the rostrum, he was denounced by the audience, many of whom even thronged onto the stage to beat him. Totally discredited, he had to slink off through a backstage exit. This was vivid evidence that the reformists were on the decline while the revolutionaries were growing strong. After it, even Liang Chi-chao's own *Hsin Min Tsung Pao* had to admit his failure.

Though the revolutionaries won the debate, their victory was far from thorough. They showed vacillation and proneness to compromise on the two basic issues of anti-imperialism and anti-feudalism. On the question of imperialist intervention, they did not dare to give a frontal response to the reformists' challenge. Instead, they argued time and again that the imperialists would refrain from crushing China for fear of upsetting the balances of power among themselves, and would have no reason for intervening against the revolution if only it confined itself to "getting rid of the Manchus" and did not touch imperialist privileges in China.

On the question of the land system and of attitude towards the masses, the revolutionaries also exhibited shortcomings. Though they had refuted the fallacious argument of the reformists that equalization of landownership would "obstruct the development of the productive forces of society," the bourgeois revolutionaries themselves did not adopt equalization of landownership as a programme of action. In fact, they had no desire at all to shake the foundations of landownership by the feudal landlord class. In their controversy with the reformists they did not lay stress on arousing the masses but on the contrary feared and tried to bind them hand and foot. They believed that only if "spontaneous rioting" by the masses was transformed into "orderly revolution," could disorder in society, and consequent imperialist intervention and partition of the country, be avoided. Such views revealed that, in their attitude towards the masses and towards imperialism, the bourgeois revolutionaries did not differ basically from the bourgeois reformists.

Armed Uprisings by Revolutionaries 6

From its founding, the China Revolutionary League called for the overthrow of the Ching government by armed uprising. In the spring of 1906 its headquarters in Tokyo sent Liu Tao-yi and Tsai Shao-nan, two Chinese students in Japan, back to Hunan to work among the Ching troops and reorganize the secret societies. Floods in the Yangtze valley area had caused a famine in which Hunan was hard hit. Landlords and big merchants seized the opportunity to raise the price of rice. The miners of the big Anyuan coalfield were near starvation and ready to revolt. Anyuan was in Pinghsiang County, Kiangsi Province, bordering on Liuyang and Liling counties in Hunan, where the secret societies had a large following. These societies had provided the basic force for the Changsha Uprising launched by the Hua Hsing Hui (Society for the Revival of the Chinese Nation) in 1904. Ma Fu-yi, one of their leaders, was arrested and executed by the Ching government in 1905. Feelings of vengeance flared, and the societies' influence spread quickly among Anyuan's miners.

Reaching Changsha, Liu Tao-yi and Tsai Shao-nan called a meeting of revolutionaries. All agreed that to seize this provincial capital it was necessary to persuade the Ching soldiers and the secret societies to rise simultaneously. It was decided to leave Liu in Changsha, in overall charge, while Tsai went to Pinghsiang to approach the secret societies in that area.

In Pinghsiang Tsai propagated the political programme of the China Revolutionary League among these organizations. He persuaded two of the larger ones to merge into the Hung Chiang Hui (Hung-kiang River Society), with Kung Chun-tai as Ta Ko ("Big Brother"). In a few months its membership grew to tens of thousands, including many Anyuan miners.

On December 3, 1906, Tsai Shao-nan and Kung Chun-tai assembled the leaders of different routes in Kaochiatai, Pinghsiang County, to discuss the time for action. Disputes arose. The next morning Liao Shu-pao, radical member of a secret society, became dissatisfied with the endless debate and went back to Liuyang County. There in a place called Mashih he assembled 2,000-3,000 people and proclaimed the uprising, hoisting a banner inscribed with a huge character, "Han." His action compelled Tsai Shao-nan, Kung Chun-tai and other leaders, in the name of the headquarters, to call on the forces of other routes to rise in support. Thus the long-pending Pinghsiang-Liuyang-Liling Uprising broke out.

Its forces took the name "The Revolutionary Vanguard of the Southern Army of the National Army of China." Kung Chun-tai was elected military governor. A proclamation declared that this army would not only overthrow the rule of the Ching nobility, break down the "several-thousand-year-old autocracy" and set up a republic. It would also "consider new laws" to "equalize landownership among the people."

Subsequently, another organization, the Hung Fu Hui (Felicity Society) in eastern and northern Liuyang County, also proclaimed an uprising. Led by Chiang Shou-tan, it called itself "The Southern Insurgent Army for the Recovery of the Great Empire of China." A third revolt was launched by secret society members in Liling, led by Li Hsiang-ko. Anyuan was decided on as the base for the insurgent forces. But the many activities of the secret societies there alerted the Ching government, which sent troops from Hunan, Hupeh, Kiangsi and

Kiangsu to suppress them. In Anyuan, soldiers blockaded the mines to prevent the workers from making contact with the outside. Nonetheless, many miners broke through to join the uprising.

Within a fortnight of its start, the Pinghsiang-Liuyang-Liling Uprising had increased its forces to 30,000 or more and gained control of four or five counties. Using crude weapons, the insurgent workers and peasants repeatedly defeated the Ching troops, seizing over 1,000 rifles. The revolution developed quickly but lacked a strong leading core. Tsai Shao-nan, a China Revolutionary League member who was one of its leaders, had no experience of war and was unable to link himself with the masses. Because of his incompetent leadership, the front and the rear each went its own way resulting in confusion. The forces of the uprising were defeated one by one under the powerful onslaughts of the counter-revolutionaries. A further cause of the failure was the lack of unity in the aim and banners of the revolutionary armies as indicated by their different names, and the consequent lack of co-ordination which weakened their fighting power.

The Pinghsiang-Liuyang-Liling Uprising had not been planned by the League headquarters. And the coded reports of it cabled by Liu Tao-yi to Japan were detained by the Changsha Telegraph Office.

So the headquarters did not even know of it until newspapers in Japan printed the news. By the time the League sent an emissary back to China, the effort had already failed and Liu Tao-yi and Tsai Shao-nan had been executed. Afterwards, the Ching government began combing the country for revolutionaries. Some League members sent back from Japan were arrested and killed, others were sentenced to lengthy imprisonment, while still others turned traitor to the revolution. When the Ching government found in the course of domiciliary searches that the directing organ of the uprising was in Japan, it asked the Tokyo government to expel Sun Yat-sen. In early 1907 Sun Yat-sen moved to Hanoi in Viet Nam, whence he sent men to start uprisings in Chaochow, Huichow, Chinchow and Lienchow in Kwangtung Province (the last two places are now included in Kwangsi). Since Chaochow and Huichow were close together, they were to rise simultaneously. But because information leaked out from among the revolutionaries at Huangkang in Chaochow, this force was compelled to rise prematurely, and thus defeated. As for the Huichow revolutionaries they were too late to respond. Though they fought for two weeks against great odds, their isolation led to failure.

After this setback, the revolutionaries started another uprising in Chinchow, captured Fangcheng and prepared to take Nanning so as to advance further into Kwangsi. The people of Chinchow and Lienchow were already in revolt against taxes, and had repeatedly defeated the Ching troops. They provided a good auxiliary to the armed struggle of the revolutionaries. But the latter, after making contact with the tax-resisters, did not organize them to extend the scope of mass struggle. Instead, they placed their hopes on a revolt by the Ching general Kuo Jen-chang. Kuo, however, proved to be a double-crosser, pretending sympathy with the revolutionary forces only to benumb the masses. Then, in a surprise stroke, he suppressed the tax-resistance struggle and, taking advantage of the fact that the revolutionary forces were blinded by illusions and detached from the masses, attacked Fang-cheng. Besieged front and rear, the revolutionaries had to withdraw to the Shihwantashan Mountains on the Kwangtung-Kwangsi border. So this struggle failed, too.

In December 1907 Sun Yat-sen and Huang Hsing staged another uprising, at Chennankuan (now Yu-yikuan) in Kwangsi where they captured the fort. But they were compelled to withdraw after seven days and nights of hard fighting.

In March 1908 Huang Hsing led a 200-man pistol unit, with overseas Chinese revolutionaries as the core, to again penetrate the Chinchow-Lienchow-

Shangszu area on the provincial border. They fought unsuccessfully for 40 days, then had to retreat. The next month the insurgent force which had retired from Chennankuan reached the border of Yunnan Province and captured Hokow, but being immediately attacked by the Ching troops had to withdraw into Viet Nam. At the request of the Ching government, the French colonial authorities there disarmed and sent them, under escort, to Singapore where they disbanded. This ended the armed struggle waged for two years by the China Revolutionary League along China's southwestern borders.

In eastern China, at about the same time, two uprisings took place in Anking, capital of Anhwei Province, led by the Kuang Fu Hui (Society for the Restoration of China). In 1907, Hsu Hsi-lin, a leader of this organization, had assassinated the provincial governor Enming, then led scores of police school cadets in a revolt. The next year Hsiung Cheng-chi, an artillery captain in a Ching garrison battalion in Anhwei, rebelled with his soldiers. In the face of great odds, both these uprisings proved shortlived. Hsu Hsi-lin had differed with Sun Yat-sen when the China Revolutionary League was set up in 1905, and in fact had refused to join the League because he regarded opposition to the Manchus as the most important objective. Later the woman revolutionary Chiu Chin joined the League and was assigned to take charge of its Chekiang Province branch. Returning home from Japan in 1906 she also joined the Kuang Fu Hui, on the recommendation of Hsu Hsi-lin, with whom she thus had two channels of contact. When Hsu started his uprising in Anking, Chiu Chin, then principal of the Tatung School in Shaohsing in Chekiang, which she had made into a revolutionary centre for armed struggle, planned to act in response as previously arranged with him. But the Anking Uprising was suppressed before Chiu Chin had fully prepared a rising in Chekiang. The Ching troops, encircling the school, arrested and murdered her.

Summing up the experience of repeated failures, the League's leaders concluded that these uprisings had been unsuccessful because the places they had selected were isolated, the transport of arms and ammunition there was difficult and because they had relied for their main force on the secret societies which had no real fighting strength. Consequently in 1909 Sun Yat-sen entrusted Huang Hsing with setting up a southern branch of the League in Hongkong. This was to concentrate on activity among the Ching government's New Army in Kwangtung Province in order to use them to start an uprising in Canton. The New Army, consisting partly of young men with some education, was trained in the last years of the Ching Dynasty by methods used in the capitalist countries and equipped with modern weapons. The actions of the revolutionaries had won the sympathy of many of the soldiers in the New Army while some had joined the League. In February 1910 Ni Ying-tien, a League member, led 3,000 New Army men in an uprising in Canton. It was put down by the Ching troops under Li Chun, Naval Commander-in-Chief in Kwangtung, Ni was killed in action and this uprising by the New Army came to nothing.

Many revolutionaries became pessimistic after this defeat. Sun Yat-sen, coming from America to Penang in Malaya, called a meeting there to boost their morale. It decided upon another, and much larger, uprising in Canton. Sun himself travelled among the overseas Chinese to solicit funds, sending others to various capitalist countries to buy arms. The League headquarters organized an 800-strong dare-to-die corps as the core of the uprising. This was composed of overseas Chinese in Southeast Asia, Chinese students in Japan and revolutionaries in China. At the same time they made contact with the New Army, the local garrison and the secret societies to muster support for the planned action. After several months' intensive preparations, the date was set for April 27, 1911.

On April 23 Huang Hsing went secretly from Hongkong to Canton where he set up a command headquarters near the office of the viceroy of Kwangtung and Kwangsi provinces and embarked on preparations. At this crucial moment the man in charge of arms deliveries turned traitor. Some weapons were lost, and the viceroy Chang Ming-chi, acting on secret information, disarmed the New Army's Second Regiment which was inclined towards the revolution and transferred three garrison battalions to reinforce Canton's defences. As the situation was getting critical for the revolutionaries, some League members wavered and asked for postponement of the uprising. Huang Hsing and others refused, but changed their plan from an advance along 10 routes to a concentrated attack on the viceroy's office.

The Canton Uprising broke out on April 27 (the 29th day of the third moon by lunar calendar) in the year 1911. Huang Hsing led over 100 fighters in the attack on the viceroy's office. They found Chang Ming-chi had already fled, and, upon emerging from the back gate, encountered Ching troops under Li Chun, Naval Commander-in-Chief in Kwangtung. Many revolutionaries were killed. Huang Hsing escaped in civilian dress. After the defeat, the people found 72 bodies of the revolutionaries killed in the battle and buried them in a common grave at Huanghuakang, on Canton's outskirts. Hence the name, Huanghuakang Uprising, used in history for this event.

The Wuchang Uprising of October 10, 1911 was preceded by no less than 10 others staged by the revolutionaries in different places. Generally they followed one of the following three patterns: (1) Transport of arms and ammunition to the forces assembled for action at a designated place, as in the 1908 uprising at Hokow in Yunnan and the 1911 Huanghuakang Uprising; (2) uprisings by Ching troops such as that at Anking led by Hsiung Chengchi in 1908 and the New Army uprising at Canton launched by Huang Hsing and others in 1910; and (3) actions leaning on the strength of the secret societies or taking the opportunity of anti-hunger and tax-resistance revolts by the people, as in the Pinghsiang-Liuyang-Liling Uprising in 1906 and the uprisings in Chaochow, Huichow, Chinchow, Lienchow and Fangcheng, all in 1907. These three patterns had a common shortcoming: in none were the masses mobilized on a large scale, and all were pure military adventures by the revolutionaries. Hence as soon as the enemy mustered for counter-attack, they were faced with great odds. Though contact was, indeed, made with the secret societies, it was only to make them instruments for purely military adventures. Very little was done to remould them, still less to arouse the masses through them. Moreover, the leadership of the secret societies was in part controlled by the landlord class, and the bourgeois revolutionaries paid attention only to making contact with these organizations so they became all the more divorced from the masses of workers and peasants.

Some of the revolutionaries having lost confidence in the future cause after so many failures, turned to assassination. If they succeeded in killing certain Manchu and Han high officials, they hoped, a turn of fortune might bring victory. The *Min Pao* (*People's Journal*), in its last few issues, kept on urging assassination, bringing the idea into great vogue. There were also people who, seeing no light ahead, grew discontented with the China Revolutionary League, bringing disunity and weakness into its leadership in the subsequent large-scale revolutionary movement.

Even though a section of the bourgeoisie and petty bourgeoisie fell into depression and wavering, the tide of mass resistance struggles swept the bourgeois-democratic revolution forward.

In his article "The Orientation of the Youth Movement," Chairman Mao said of China's democratic revolution: **"What is its main force? The common people of China. The motive forces of the revolution are the proletariat, the peasantry and all members of other classes who are willing to oppose imperialism and feudalism; these are the revolutionary forces opposing imperialism and feudalism. But who, among so many, are the basic force, the backbone of the revolution? The workers and the peasants, forming 90 per cent of the country's population."**

From the time of its birth, the Chinese working class stood at the forefront of the anti-imperialist and anti-feudal struggle.

China's working class was born in the 1840s. Its emergence and growth accompanied not only that of the Chinese national bourgeoisie, but also that of the imperialist-run enterprises in China. This being so, a large section of the Chinese working class had a longer history than the Chinese national bourgeoisie, as well as greater social strength and a larger social base. As China's national capitalism began to develop, and foreign industrial establishments on her soil grew in number, the ranks of the Chinese working class gradually expanded. Before the Revolution of 1911 there were 500,000-600,000 industrial workers in the whole country, a very small percentage of the population. But China's working class represented the advanced productive forces. It was concentrated and subject to the triple oppression of imperialism, feudalism and capitalism. Hence it was thoroughly revolutionary and particularly militant.

In 1884 when Sun Yat-sen, pioneer of China's bourgeois-democratic revolution, was beginning to work out his revolutionary ideas, he was already deeply impressed by the working-class struggle against imperialist aggression. In September of that year a French warship damaged while invading

China's Taiwan and Fukien came to Hongkong for repairs. Chinese shipyard workers there downed tools and refused the job. And when French merchant vessels entered Hongkong, the Chinese dockers refused to unload them, and porters and carters joined in the strike. British colonial authorities in Hongkong sent troops to suppress the strikers, arresting 30 and killing one. The unarmed workers fought back, wounding more than 10 of the British. After these clashes, Hongkong's Chinese workers struck again, shopkeepers closed their doors and even the rice-hullers declared a stoppage. Quickly the movement spread to Kowloon. The British aggressors were compelled to release the arrested workers. And the ships of French aggressors, unable to get food in Hongkong, had to sail off to Saigon for it. Sun Yat-sen, then studying in Hongkong, was greatly inspired when he saw this.

As time passed and modern social contradictions in China grew sharper, spontaneous working-class struggles multiplied. From 1895 to 1913, more than 90 strikes broke out in Shanghai alone. In 1897, some 5,000 wheelbarrow-men fought one against license fees imposed on them in Shanghai's foreign concessions. At one point it rose to the pitch of revolt, and the workers used sticks, carrying-poles, bricks and stones against the police. Although it was suppressed by British and American imperialist marines the outbreak showed the fighting spirit of the first generation of Shanghai transport workers.

Struggles also occurred in another industrial centre, Wuhan (the triple city of Wuchang, Hankow and Hanyang). In 1905 a strike of over 3,000 coppersmiths was called in Hankow, against capitalists who had reduced wages on some pretext. In 1907, workers at the mint for copper coins in the same city struck against a cut in their wage. In 1909, in brick-tea factories run by foreign capital in Hankow, 8,000-9,000 workers walked out to protest exploitation by contract-labour bosses and demand a wage rise. The foreign capitalists rejected their demand. The thousands of militant workers gave the bosses a beating. In January 1911, also in Hankow, a British concession police detective savagely kicked a ricksha-puller to death. Public indignation flared up. The next day more than 1,000 ricksha-men assembled in front of the British police station demanding punishment of the murderer. The British consul ordered his soldiers to fire, killing more than 10 Chinese workers. Chang Piao, commander of the Ching troops in Hankow, and Chi Yao-shan, Intendant of the Kianghankuan Circuit, appeared on the scene with 5,000 soldiers, and ordered the throng to disperse. The angry demonstrators surrounded and beat Chi Yao-shan, injuring him in the left eye. Later people from all walks of life in Wuhan, numbering tens of thousands, met in unanimous protest against British imperialist savagery and the Ching government's treachery. But Chang Piao, to protect his foreign masters, stationed himself in the British concession and sent out soldiers every day to patrol its perimeter and guard the streets on which the foreigners lived, as well as all churches outside the concession. In this way the Ching authorities used brute force to suppress the mass protest. But the more openly the Ching rulers stood with the imperialists, the more they cut themselves off from the people. A revolutionary situation in the triple city was ripening.

However, in the period before the Revolution of 1911, the Chinese working class did not yet appear on the political arena as an awakened and independent class force. Struggles by the masses of workers were spontaneous and scattered; they took part in the revolution as followers of the bourgeoisie and petty bourgeoisie. Its main and hardest-fighting force still consisted of the poor and lower-middle peasants. In the late 19th century, with imperialist aggression making deeper inroads in China, the peasant masses continued along the course set by the Taiping revolutionary war which had struck heavy blows at feudal rule. Spontaneously, they raised the banner of opposition to the foreign churches. This later developed into the Yi Ho Tuan

73

Movement against the imperialist plot to partition China, marking another revolutionary upsurge in modern Chinese history with the peasants making up the main force. After the failure of the Yi Ho Tuan Movement, the bourgeois-led democratic revolution made vigorous headway while anti-church struggle was relegated to a secondary role.

However, between 1901 and 1908 incidents of "burning of churches and killing of missionaries" continued to occur. During these struggles against the foreign churches, it should be noted, slogans such as "oppose the Ching and exterminate the foreigners" were openly raised, and activities which the Ching government called "abominating the churches and killing officials" were common. This shows that the people had learned a lesson from the failure of the Yi Ho Tuan Movement and begun, though still spontaneously, to link their fight against imperialism with their fight against feudalism.

One form of the peasant resistance to feudal rule was refusal to pay taxes and levies. This traditional mode of revolt against oppression rose to new heights in the early 20th century. Riots exploded far and wide — in Hsiangfu in Honan Province, Taichow in Kiangsu Province, Wuchow in Kwangsi Province, Yuncheng in Shantung Province and elsewhere. Many government offices and tax-collection posts were attacked and wrecked. In 1904 the people of Loping County, Kiangsi Province, rose against a tax on indigo. They kept their fight going for six months and on one occasion occupied the county seat. There they seized arms and destroyed the magistrate's office and those of the salt revenue, inland transit tax and other tax services along with the foreign churches, thus striking a severe blow at the Ching rulers and duly punishing the foreign aggressors. Even more extensive was the tax-resistance movement in Laiyang, Shantung, in 1910. Some 60,000 insurgents under Chu Shih-wen, leader of a federation of eight villages, combed the locality, making captives of the local despots and evil gentry who had robbed the people with heavy levies in the name of "reforms." The Shantung governor sent a large force to suppress the uprising. The troops killed many people and burned hundreds of houses. The Ching government's policy of savage massacre only aroused fiercer mass resistance, thus hastening its downfall. The flame of the Laiyang people's revolt spread quickly to neighbouring counties.

At about the same time rice riots broke out in the Yangtze valley. Between 1907 and 1910, over 90 hunger-uprisings occurred in many sub-prefectures and counties of Hunan, Hupeh, Kiangsi, Anhwei and Kiangsu provinces along the middle and lower reaches of the river. Widest in its repercussions was the rice riot in Changsha, Hunan, in 1910. A flood in 1909 had reduced the grain crop. More than 100,000 people in the province faced starvation. The officials, gentry, rich businessmen and foreign firms took advantage of the disaster to hoard grain and push up its price. Life became impossible for the peasants, handicraftsmen, railway workers and townsfolk. In April 1910, a water carrier in Changsha drowned himself, with his entire family, because he could not buy a tenth of a peck of rice with his wage for a long hard day's work. The tragedy aroused the people to fury. Thousands took to the streets, raiding the hulling mills, rice shops, money houses, tax-collecting stations, foreign consulates, foreign firms and churches, and setting fire to the governor's own office. This revolutionary storm shook the entire country, posing a direct threat to the Ching Dynasty's rule.

Stirred by mass struggle of the workers and peasants, ordinary townsfolk and a section of the national capitalists joined its ranks. In 1905 alone, there were over 80 mass risings, of which more than 20 were strikes staged by businessmen and other urban dwellers. At this same juncture, a boycott of American goods developed into a nationwide patriotic movement, dealing a heavy blow to U.S. imperialism.

The U.S.A. was a late-comer among capitalist countries. The mines, railroads and cities in its western states were built largely with the sweat and blood of Chinese labourers. When the American capitalists needed labour power, they did not stop at deception, smuggling or even kidnapping to bring a large number of Chinese workers into the United States. But when a capitalist economic crisis arose they tried to divert the spearhead of the American workers' struggle against the Chinese labourers, maliciously charging them with taking the bread out of the mouths of American workers and stirring up anti-Chinese agitation and outrages. These kindled the Chinese people's hatred against the U.S. government. When the Sino-American treaty, which discriminated against the Chinese labourers and had been forced upon the Ching government, was due to expire in December 1904, the Chinese people at home and overseas demanded its abrogation. The U.S. government, however, refused to negotiate about this. In May 1905 a section of Shanghai's national bourgeoisie who had suffered losses from the influx of American manufactures sent out a circular appealing for a country-wide boycott of such goods. Quick response came from the business organizations of cities and towns all over China, and from a number of overseas Chinese trading groups. Thus arose a movement unprecedented in modern Chinese history, directed against the United States. Most persistent were the worker and peasant masses. U.S. imperialism received a heavy blow — the import of American goods to China went down drastically between 1905 and 1907.

The patriotic movement against the U.S., in its turn, pushed forward the struggles for recovery of mining and railway rights in various provinces. The people of Shansi had struggled since 1898 to recover their coal and iron ore mining rights, appropriated by British capitalists. In 1907, after many twists and turns, they finally kicked out the British aggressors and set up a mining corporation to operate the mines by local effort. Two years later the people of Anhwei took back the Tungkuanshan coal mine from British commercial interests. However, after the people had reclaimed these mining and railway rights, the Ching government again sold them to foreigners. Struggles over such issues inevitably became a component of the revolution.

The Ching Government's Sham Constitutionalism

8

Mass revolts and waves of democratic revolution increasingly threatened the reactionary Ching regime. Seeing that their counter-revolutionary aim could not be achieved by the policy of barbarous massacre, the Ching rulers resorted to peaceful deception to benumb the people. The sham constitutionalism of the dynasty's last years was of this description.

After suppressing the great Yi Ho Tuan Movement in collusion with the allied army of the eight imperialist powers, the Ching government signed the Protocol of 1901, going further in selling out the country and people than ever before. Thereby it threw itself into the arms of the imperialists. And "Down with the traitorous Ching government" became the common call of the people of all China's nationalities including a section of the medium and small landlords. In order to appease the angry masses the Empress Dowager Tzu Hsi, taking refuge in Sian after the imperialist invaders had driven her from Peking, hastily and hypocritically issued a rescript of "Self-Blame" in the emperor's name and set up a "Political Affairs Supervisory Office" to carry out "reforms." This inaugurated the Ching court's policy of peaceful deception. Between 1901 and 1905 scores of "reforms" were rigged up but they did not go beyond "abolishing the imperial examinations, establishing schools and sending students abroad." These points were plagiarized from the Reform Movement of 1898 which the Ching rulers themselves had repudiated, but were now using to cheat the people.

Despite this loud "reform" fanfare of the Ching rulers, the bourgeois-led democratic revolution surged forward. In the face of the political offensive by the revolutionaries and under the pressure of public opinion, the bourgeois reformists, who had degenerated into monarchists, immediately took fright. Particularly on tenterhooks were their leaders, Kang Yu-wei, Liang Chi-chao and the like. They kept urging the Ching rulers to institute a constitutional monarchy as quickly as possible, so as to block the advance of the revolutionary forces.

The reformists' programme had the support of a section of landlords and officials who were just then turning into bourgeois. These types came to be called the constitutionalists — more accurately, they were constitutional monarchists.

In 1903 Chang Chien of Kiangsu Province and Tang Shou-chien of Chekiang Province had begun to draw up constitutional plans. In the following year they entered into collaboration with certain provincial officials — Viceroy Wei Kuang-tao of Kiangsu, Anhwei and Kiangsi; Viceroy Chang Chih-tung of Hupeh and Hunan, and Viceroy Yuan Shih-kai of Chihli (now Hopei Province) — in the hope that memorials advocating constitutional monarchy would be submitted to the Ching court in the name of these potentates. When Japan defeated Russia in the Russo-Japanese War in 1905, the constitutionalists used that event to work on public opinion. They said that Japan had won because she was a constitutional monarchy, Russia had lost because she was a tsarist autocracy, and autocracy had brought upon Russia not only defeat in the war with Japan but also revolution within the country. So, they argued, the only way to both strengthen China and prevent revolution was constitutional monarchy.

In 1905, at the urging of the constitutionalists, Sun Pao-chi, the Ching government's Minister Plenipotentiary to France, presented the first petition for governmental reform. Then followed others, by Chou Fu, Viceroy of Kiangsu, Anhwei and Kiangsi, Chang Chih-tung, Viceroy of Hupeh and Hunan, Tsen Chun-hsuan, Acting Viceroy of Kwangtung and Kwangsi, Yuan Shih-kai, Viceroy of Chihli, and so on. These landowning bureaucrats of Han nationality became interested in constitutional monarchy mainly because they were discontented with the monopoly of power in the Ching court by a small number of nobles of the imperial clan. Through a constitutional government, they themselves hoped to replace these nobles, if not altogether then at least in part.

Under pressure of the revolutionary situation, the Empress Dowager accepted their views and sent a mission of five high ministers, headed by Tsaitse, abroad to study constitutional government. The court would adopt this form of government, she said, if the mission's studies proved that it could really "stabilize the foundation of the Ching Dynasty forever," and "automatically wipe out talk of revolution."

The constitutionalists were beside themselves with joy at the news of this mission. "A great event!" they exclaimed.

To head off this swindle by the Ching court, Wu Yueh, a revolutionary, took a bomb to the Peking railway station, intending to assassinate the five envoys as they left. But when he stepped on the train the bomb exploded in the crowd. Two of the envoys were lightly wounded. Wu himself was killed.

Upon their return to China in 1906, the five envoys petitioned the court to institute constitutional government. In a confidential memorial to the Empress Dowager, Tsaitse listed three advantages of doing so: "Permanent stabilization of imperial rule; gradual mitigation of the menace from foreign powers; and prevention of internal disturbances." Moreover, he added slyly, after constitutional government was proclaimed, its actual establishment could still be put off. The Meiji Restoration in Japan provided an example. Constitutional government there was announced in the 14th year of Meiji's reign, but it was only in the 23rd year that the Diet was convened. The interval of eight to nine years afforded plenty of leeway. The Empress Dowager gave several individual audiences to the five envoys. In addition, she called "conferences before the emperor." The conclusion from these repeated consultations was that sham constitutionalism would really help stabilize the Ching rule. On September 1, 1906, an imperial edict was issued on preparation for "adoption of a constitutional government on Western pattern." Thus the constitutional fraud was officially launched.

In fact, this edict was a clear example of the fact that no reactionary ruling class ever gives up the least bit of political power of its own accord.

It laid down the guiding principle for the preparation of a constitutional government as follows: "State power to be concentrated in the court and state affairs to be open to public opinion, so as to secure a lasting moral base for the state." However, said the edict, the system was not yet perfect nor the people sufficiently educated; so constitutional government could not come immediately. It was necessary first to reform the administrative system, make laws, widely develop education, adjust finance, improve national defence, institute a nation-wide police system . . . and after several years decide on the time to enforce constitutional government in the light of the situation then. In the interval, it continued, government officials and people must be loyal to the sovereign and patriotic, respect order and preserve peace so as to "qualify" themselves as citizens of a constitutional state.

Clearly the Ching government was prepared to give the people a paper constitution in the far-off future provided they stop opposing the regime. But if they continued to oppose it, they would be regarded as "rebels against the authorities," unfit to be citizens of a constitutional state, and would receive not a constitution but cruel suppression.

In short, the edict was a rubber cheque, a fraud on the people.

This sham cooked up by the Ching court, however, had the support of the constitutionalists at home and abroad. In December 1906, Kang Yu-wei published a statement in the *Chung Kuo Wei Hsin* (*China Reform*), a paper published in New York, notifying monarchist associations in different places to transform themselves, beginning January 1, 1907, into "Citizens' Constitutional Associations" — political bodies for the promotion of constitutional government. Liang Chi-chao, on his part, founded the Cheng Wen Sheh (Political Information Association) in Tokyo, and issued statements and drew up programmes in support of the Ching government's announcement; besides which he sent people back to China for contact. But despite the attempts of Kang, Liang and their like to curry favour with the Ching court, the Empress Dowager could not forget her grudge against them for their role in the Reform Movement of 1898. Saying that they were "protecting the emperor but not the Empress Dowager, protecting China but not the Ching Dynasty," she issued orders for the arrest of Kang, Liang and their followers, and would not permit them to come out in public. As these exiles were blocked, constitutionalists within the country like Chang Chien,

Tang Shou-chien, Tang Hua-lung and Tan Yen-kai took their place as leaders. Collaborating with a section of local officials and gentry, they formed associations in Kiangsu, Chekiang, Hupeh, Hunan and Kwangtung provinces under various names — Union for Preparing Constitutional Government, Constitution Preparatory Union, Constitutional Union, Autonomy Association, and so on. All were mere cheering squads for the Ching rulers' sham constitutionalism.

In 1908 the Union for Preparing Constitutional Government led by Chang Chien in Kiangsu sponsored a petition to the Ching court. Chang was a *Chuang Yuan* (top graduate in the palace examination conducted personally by the emperor) who had sympathized with the 1898 Reform Movement. He had since become a big textile and flour-milling capitalist. Now he emerged as the overall domestic leader of the constitutionalists, and invited their representatives from the provinces to come to Peking and petition for early convocation of a parliament. Between the Ching government and the constitutionalists there was collusion as well as struggle — collusion because both wanted to use the constitutional fraud to prevent revolution; struggle because they had some conflicts of interest. The constitutionalists hoped, through the reform, to set limits on the diehard forces in the

Ching court in order to worm their own way into its organs of state power. The diehards of the imperial clan, on their part, would permit no change which might hamper their own sway. And they themselves were trying to manipulate constitutional government as a means of concentrating power in the imperial household, leaving the Han landlord-bureaucrats out in the cold. Each side having its own designs, a dog-eat-dog fight was inevitable.

While the Ching government and the constitutionalists fought each other both openly and secretly, a succession of mass struggles against brutal suppression, co-ordinated with armed uprisings by the revolutionaries, hammered at the Ching regime. Some members of its ruling circles were scared out of their wits. As the revolutionary tide mounted, even the most diehard began to feel that "the only way to prevent revolution is constitutionalism." So they decided to win over the constitutionalists as allies in counter-revolution. In 1908 the Ching government promulgated the "Regulations for Provincial Consultative Assemblies" and later the "General Principles of the Constitution Approved by His Majesty." It laid down a preparatory period of nine years before the constitution would come into effect, a definite time limit instead of the formerly unlimited one.

The "General Principles" contained 14 articles prescribing the powers of the emperor, all those of a typical feudal monarch, and nine on the duties of the officials and people, including the payment of taxes and military service. The Ching court was merely using the name constitutional government to practise absolute monarchy. The so-called preparatory period was but its counter-revolutionary cover.

The Kuang Hsu Emperor and the Empress Dowager died soon after the "General Principles" were proclaimed. The three-year-old Puyi was elevated to the throne under the reign-title of Hsuan Tung. The year 1909 was thus called the First Year of Hsuan Tung. The prince regent Tsaifeng, the child's father, continued the constitutional farce while gradually seizing back power from, and reducing the functions of, the Han warlords and landlords. Fearing that Yuan Shih-kai's power would be detrimental to the imperial house, the Ching rulers ordered him to return to his home town, Changteh, in Honan Province to "rest" on account of a "foot ailment." Their scheme was to save the Ching Dynasty by concentrating power in the imperial house.

These perversities antagonized the constitutionalists, who were already dissatisfied with the "General Principles," and particularly the nine-year preparatory period. They were afraid that long postponement might turn into breach of promise, after which there would be no way to stem the revolutionary tide. They also had a fellow-feeling for the plight of Yuan Shih-kai and the others who had been shorn of power, which made them uncertain of their own political future. So they decided to put up a fight. At Chang Chien's suggestion, they formed the "Association of Petitioners for a Parliament" and in February 1910 went in a group to Peking to urge the Ching government quickly to convene parliament and organize a cabinet. All their 10 petitions were rejected. The breach between the constitutionalists and the Ching government became more apparent.

In October 1910 the Ching government set up the Central Consultative Assembly. Some constitutionalists were selected as members, which widened their sphere of activity. Seizing this advantage, their colleagues in different provinces joined forces and, working with some of the viceroys and governors who gave them support, again petitioned the court. But the ruling clique refused to make any concession. On the contrary, it ordered the representatives from the three northeastern provinces sent back under escort and exiled one from Chihli Province to Sinkiang, as a warning to other would-be petitioners. Thus the dominant clique showed its unwillingness to give up even a jot of political power, or allow the provincial officials any more power and influence on any pretext. The contradiction between the Ching government and the constitutionalists widened in scope.

In May 1911, to fulfil its earlier promise to form a "responsible cabinet" as the first step, the Ching government issued an edict of administrative reform. A cabinet list of 13 members was announced — consisting of a prime minister, deputy prime ministers and ministers — of whom eight would be Manchu nobles, one a Mongol noble and four Han officials. Such a cabinet, concentrating power in the hands of the members of the imperial house to the virtual exclusion of the Han landowner-bureaucrats, was a further disappointment to the constitutionalists. Aiming to hold off the revolution, they continued to urge the Ching government to change its opposition-breeding ways. In July the provincial consultative assemblies petitioned for the rescinding of the cabinet edict. Again, they drew a rejection, with which the constitutionalists' hope of a seat in the cabinet vanished. Consequently, with their members in the Central Consultative Assembly as the core, they organized the "Friends of the Constitution Society," the "Association for Advancing Constitutional Government" and the "1911 Club." These groups had the nature of political parties. Through them, the constitutionalists were prepared on the one hand to continue bargaining with the Ching government and on the other opportunistically to join the revolution if it came.

The Ching government had intended to use its sham reform to win over the constitutionalists in order to oppose the revolution and maintain its own reactionary rule. The result was the opposite of its wishes. The revolutionary forces were not weakened, the court exposed itself, got into a deadlock with the constitutionalists, lost supporters and became increasingly isolated. The constitutionalists had been the Ching government's parrots to start with. But their minor contradictions with it — elements of contention alongside their collusion — gave them some political capital with which to hoodwink the people. After the Revolution of 1911 they wormed their way into the revolutionary ranks for sabotage from within. Their termite-like wrecking was in part responsible for the failure of the 1911 Revolution.

The repeated blatant rejection of the constitutionalists' demands by the Ching government was inseparably linked with foreign imperialist support for the regime. The first action of the imperial cabinet after it was formed, therefore, was to declare the "nationalization of railways," in the name of which railway-building rights were taken away from the provinces and auctioned off to imperialism. The railway companies formed in several provinces had been mainly controlled by constitutionalists, whose interests were thus the first to be affected by "nationalization." Therefore they started an agitation on the railway question. Their plan was to use the strength of the masses to pressure the Ching government into a deal and thus hanging on to part of the railway shares. But once the masses arose, the constitutionalists could not control them. The agitation, gaining momentum, became the prelude to the fall of the Ching rule. This was much more than the constitutionalists had bargained for.

Why did the railway agitation become a large-scale mass movement? There were profound historical reasons. At the end of the 19th century the imperialists were daily stepping up their plunder of China. They expanded their spheres of influence mainly by robbing China of more and more of her sovereign rights and exporting capital to China — thus gaining control of her economic lifelines. A major means of their economic plunder was to grab the right to make loans (or direct investments) for railway-building. For such loans (or investments) were not only highly profitable but could endow the lenders (or investors) with rights of management, control over trade, mining, forestry and tele-communications enterprises along the railway lines, and even such privileges as setting up tax-collection posts, and the stationing and transport of their own troops. Thus, the spheres of influence of the imperialist powers expanded along with their control of China's railways.

Because contention for railway rights was so important a part of the imperialist policies of aggression, U.S. imperialism, as a late-comer, devoted particular attention to it. In 1896, it set up the American China Development Company, chiefly for the seizure of railway-building rights. First fastening its eyes on the route between Canton and Hankow, it planned to grab the construction rights for a line there through action by the Ching government. In Hunan Province, which lay along this route, the gentry-merchants (that is, landowner-bureaucrats who were turning into bourgeois, or members of the upper bourgeoisie closely linked with the landowning officials) were trying to extend their own economic influence. Jointly with their counterparts in the two other provinces involved, Hupeh and Kwangtung, they petitioned the Ching government for permission to build the Canton-Hankow Railway themselves. But the Ching court was busy selling mining, railway and territorial rights to the imperialists, having entered into collusion with them to maintain its tottering reactionary rule. Naturally it ignored the request of the gentry-merchants of these three provinces. In April 1898 and July 1900, with the big compradore Sheng Hsuan-huai doing the manipulating, it signed the "Draft Contract for the Canton-Hankow Railway Loan" with the American China Development Company, plus a "Supplementary Agreement," selling the construction rights for this line to U.S. imperialism.

Just then, the mighty Yi Ho Tuan Movement broke out in north China, striking a severe blow at the evil aggressions of the imperialists in China. The U.S. imperialists, after cunningly obtaining the building rights for the Canton-Hankow rail line, were afraid the people along the route might rise in opposition. So they dared not start full-scale construction and later, they sold two-thirds of the shares to Belgian interests on the international market, at a big profit.

In the face of U.S. imperialism's sly contravention of the "Supplementary Agreement for the Canton-Hankow Railway Loan" the people of Hunan, Hupeh and Kwangtung rose in a movement demanding its abrogation. Together with the boycott of American goods which began that same year, this movement spread far and wide. U.S. imperialism was compelled temporarily to relinquish its attempt to monopolize the construction rights for the line and agree to cancel the contract. But it still would not withdraw its claws, and compelled the Ching government to "redeem" the 30 kilometres or more of the rail line already built at the exorbitant price of some four million U.S. dollars.

With the recovery of the right to build the Canton-Hankow Railway, companies were set up in Hunan, Hupeh and Kwangtung to raise funds for its construction. A portion was invested by the gentry-merchants. But the larger part was extracted from the masses of working people. The methods used were: purchase of shares with funds raised from the inland transit tax on rice and salt, "land rent shares" allotting a percentage of land rents for the purpose, shares paid for by a set percentage of wages earned, and shares subscribed for by the people directly and voluntarily. All this made the question of railway rights the common concern of persons in many different walks of life in the three provinces.

The imperialist aggressors would not reconcile themselves to the fact that this trunk railway, crossing three provinces, was coming under the control of the Chinese people. And the handful of reactionaries who comprised the Ching government would not give up their peddling China's sovereign rights. So under-cover bargaining for this railway continued. Even while the "redemption" of the already-built section was being negotiated, Chang Chih-tung, Viceroy of Hupeh and Hunan, took action under the Ching court's orders to "prepare for the recovery of the Canton-Hankow Railway rights" and approached Britain for a loan on the pretext that the "redemption" funds were difficult to raise at home. As a quid pro quo, he promised the British priority rights to invest in the building of the line, thus turning over to Britain the sovereign rights of China which had just been recovered from the Americans. In 1908, the Ching government appointed Chang Chih-tung as "High Commissioner to Supervise the Canton-Hankow Railway" at the instigation of the imperialists to negotiate a construction loan with the latter. In 1910 the "Agreement for the Hukuang Railway Loan" was signed with Britain, Germany and France. U.S. imperialism was angered at seeing the construction rights for the Canton-Hankow line falling into the hands of these three rivals. U.S. President Taft personally wrote to the Ching government applying direct pressure and starting a dispute with the other powers. Finally in May of the same year an agreement for a four-power consortium including the U.S.A. was reached in Paris. The right to build the Canton-Hankow Railway, which the people of the three provinces had fought to recover, was again officially sold to foreign aggressors.

Because the Ching government had an understanding with imperialism, the cabinet declared the nationalization of the railways as one of its very first acts using the strong medium of a rescript issued in the name of the Hsuan Tung Emperor. Tuanfang was appointed "High Commissioner to Supervise the Canton-Hankow and Szechuan-Hankow Railways," and ordered to take over the provincial railway companies in Hupeh, Hunan,

Kwangtung and Szechuan. The clique of traitors in the Ching government used the pretext of railway-building to contract many foreign loans by which they corruptly enriched themselves. And under the signboard of "nationalization of railways" they wrested the railway investments from Chinese businessmen and other sections of the people. They thought happily that they were killing two birds with one stone, oblivious of the fact that their reactionary ways were arousing more opposition from the people, and angering even the constitutionalists who had hitherto supported them. They were rushing down an ever-narrowing road.

First to rise against the emperor's rescript were the gentry-merchants in Hunan. Meeting at the provincial consultative assembly building they distributed leaflets exposing the Ching government's criminal contracting of large foreign loans and sell-out of the country's sovereign rights. Students quit their classes to protest, and the struggle intensified. Fearing the spread of popular indignation, Yang Wen-ting, Governor of Hunan, memorialized the emperor for the rescinding of the nationalization order. He was severely reprimanded and ordered to suppress the mass struggle instead. In Hupeh Province the fight was more acute. The revolutionary Chan Ta-pei wrote an article advocating revolution in the *Ta Chiang Pao* (*Great River News*), entitled "Great Disorder Is the Cure for China." Juicheng, Viceroy of Hupeh and Hunan, had Chan arrested and the paper closed. Thousands of people held a meeting in the provincial consultative assembly building, and one man cut off his own finger to show determination, amid weeping and shouts of "Save the country!" They sent delegates with a petition to Peking, where they went on a hunger strike lasting three days and nights. In Kwangtung, the shareholders of the railway company of that province unanimously denounced the nationalization and, in protest, refused to use the Ching government's paper currency. Placed under heavy pressure they had to flee to Hongkong, where they organized the Pao Lu Hui (Protect-the-Railway Society) and continued their struggle, obtaining support from the *Chung Kuo Jih Pao* (*China Daily*), run by the China Revolutionary League, and other papers in that city. This so frightened Chang Mingchi, Viceroy of Kwangtung and Kwangsi, that he banned the import of newspapers from Hongkong.

In Szechuan the railway agitation was wider, deeper and more protracted.

The Szechuan-Hankow Railway Company in that province had been established in 1904. The British and French imperialists had been attempting for some time to seize construction rights for this line but failed because of popular opposition.

In 1909 when the Ching government sold out the Canton-Hankow line rights for the second time, it also sold those of the Szechuan-Hankow Railway. The "Agreement for the Hukuang Railway Loan" covered not only the former line but the Hupeh section of the latter. In fact, the Ching regime had auctioned off all the railway rights in Kwangtung, Szechuan, Hunan and Hupeh and, on the basis of this agreement, ordered their local railway companies taken over by High Commissioner Tuanfang. When the emperor's rescript reached Szechuan, shareholders in Chengtu met and set up the Pao Lu Tung Chih Hui (Association of Comrades for Protecting the Railway), with the constitutionalist leaders Pu Tien-chun and Lo Lun as chairman and vice-chairman.

Though started by the constitutionalists, this association was an open organization, a fact that facilitated the entry of the masses into the struggle to protect the railway. As for the Szechuan Railway Company itself, though it too was then controlled by the constitutionalists and other members of the upper strata, its source of funds was largely from the lower strata of society, the working people. They showed high enthusiasm in this fight and joined the association in large numbers.

Less than a fortnight after its birth, the association had 100,000 members engaged in ardent struggle. The constitutionalists took fright, trying their utmost to limit the movement to the submission of memorials and petitions. But the Ching government, instead of being moved by their supplications, appointed Chao Erh-feng, Viceroy of Szechuan, to undertake suppression. Chao Erh-feng was known as the "murderous demon-king." In the spring of 1904, as Intendant of the Yungning Circuit in Szechuan, he had slaughtered more than 3,000 peasants in Hsuyung County within two months for their resistance to taxes. For his heinous crime Chao had been promoted to the post of High Commissioner for Szechuan-Yunnan Border Affairs. So the people of Szechuan hated him bitterly. The news of his appointment as provincial viceroy, and his coming forward to suppress the railway agitation, infuriated the masses.

In August 1911 the Ching government forcibly took over the section of the Szechuan-Hankow Railway line between Ichang (in Hupeh Province) and Wanhsien (in Szechuan). When the news reached Chengtu the railway company shareholders, then meeting there, exploded in anger. Jointly with the members of the Pao Lu Tung Chih Hui they held a mass rally of tens of thousands of people. They called for protest strikes, shopkeepers closed their doors and students walked out of their classes. Such actions spread from Chengtu to

Szechuan's other sub-prefectures and counties. Every day the press reported riots by the poor, raids on the tax bureaus, police stations and foreign churches, and armed clashes with the police. The situation was developing excellently. On September 1 the masses declared that they would not pay taxes in grain or cash, nor a single cent for defraying foreign debts. This fight against taxes and levies pushed the railway protection movement further forward.

Szechuan was a rich source of extortion for the Ching government. So its masses' refusal to pay taxes and levies upset the court, which hastily sent Tuanfang with troops from Hupeh to suppress them. Chao Erh-feng was also ordered to take repressive measures, in a vain attempt to extinguish the flames of mass struggle.

On September 7 Chao Erh-feng arrested the railway company leaders, Pu Tien-chun and Lo Lun. The people rushed to the viceroy's office to demand their release. Chao ordered his soldiers to open fire, killing 32 city people and scores of peasants who had come from the outskirts to give them support. This was the famous Chengtu massacre.

After this, local members of the China Revolutionary League made a large number of wooden boards inscribed with the words: "First Chao Erh-feng arrested Pu Tien-chun and Lo Lun; next he will crush Szechuan. Comrades everywhere, rise at once to save yourselves!" The boards, varnished with tung oil and wrapped in oil-paper, were thrown into the Chingkiang River. They came to be known as "water telegrams." As they floated downstream, the people picked them up and knowledge of Chao Erh-feng's atrocities flashed throughout southeastern Szechuan. A province-wide armed uprising then broke out. Lung Ming-chien of the China Revolutionary League, acting jointly with the Ko Lao Hui (Society of Brothers), organized the Army of Comrades for Railway Protection. It besieged Chengtu, fought battles in many other places and occupied several sub-prefectures and counties. On September 25 Wu Yu-chang, Wang Tien-chieh and others declared the independence of Junghsien County where they set up revolutionary power. The revolution in Szechuan stimulated the development of the revolutionary situation throughout China. And the Ching government's transfer of a part of the army to Szechuan, from Hupeh, weakened reactionary rule in the latter province, providing favourable conditions for the impending Wuchang Uprising.

In the wake of the surging railway agitation in Hupeh, Hunan, Kwangtung and Szechuan provinces, the bourgeois revolutionaries in Hupeh began actively to prepare an armed uprising. Their energetic work made the triple city of Wuhan an important breakthrough point for the 1911 Revolution.

Around the time of the founding of the China Revolutionary League in 1905, capitalist industry and commerce were developing to a certain degree and the struggle between new and old ideas was sharp in Kwangtung, Hupeh, Hunan and provinces along the lower Yangtze. Activities by revolutionaries quickly made these areas into centres of bourgeois-democratic revolution. Wuhan was a very important one.

Wuhan's importance was due to objective conditions there and the subjective efforts of the revolutionaries.

The objective conditions were: class and national contradictions were sharp and the mass base for the revolution was strong.

At the end of the 19th and the beginning of the 20th century, the imperialists extended their forces of aggression to the interior of China. Wuhan was one of the centres from which they carried on plunder. Statistics show that the value of foreign trade through Hankow rose from 50 million ounces of silver in 1898 to 100 million in 1902 and 150 million in 1910 — trebling in 12 years and making it the country's largest trading port after Shanghai. Through this place, imperialist countries dumped their goods and frenziedly grabbed low-cost raw materials, bringing endless suffering upon the people of inland China.

With the deepening of imperialist aggression, the feudal rulers turned more rapidly into compradore lackeys of foreign interests. When Chang Chih-tung became Viceroy of Hupeh and Hunan in 1889, he turned Hupeh into a centre for launching his "Westernization" or "learn from foreigners" movement, setting up munition and other industries in this province. Chang admitted that in the enterprises he founded, "everything was imported" — not only all the machinery and technical personnel, but "even the iron frames of factory buildings, iron pillars, foundations, furnace bases, cement, fireclay and so on." Part of the capital was also borrowed from abroad. So from the very beginning, these enterprises were controlled by foreign countries, and appendages to foreign monopoly capital. "Bringing the wolf into the house," Chang Chih-tung and his like threw open the gates to imperialist economic, political and cultural penetration, pushing the people of inland China ever deeper into the abyss of semi-colonialism.

The broad masses of the peasantry were the first victims of this close collusion between reactionaries at home and abroad. Chen Kuei-lung, who succeeded Chang Chih-tung as Viceroy of Hupeh and Hunan in 1909, wrote in a memorial to the emperor, "Recently with the imperial court's efforts at self-strengthening, public expenditure has multiplied many times." By "self-strengthening" he meant carrying out "Westernization" or "reforms." And the "multiplied expenditure," converted into a variety of taxes, finally fell on the shoulders of the people in town and country and especially of the peasant masses.

With the disintegration of the natural economy, many big landlords in Hupeh took up trade or opened money houses, which became a part of the imperialist network of commercial usury. Through land rent they robbed the peasants of over half of their produce, and by buying cheap, selling dear and extending pre-harvest loans they plundered raw materials for the imperialists, battening on the sweat and blood of the poor and lower-middle peasants, whom they plunged into destitution. All this seriously undermined the productive forces in the countryside. Early in the 20th century, because water conservancy works in Hupeh Province had fallen into disrepair, flood and famine occurred there yearly. The affected districts became a watery expanse, without a human habitation for many kilometres. Refugees thronged into the cities — over 200,000 came to Hankow on one occasion alone, swelling its army of unemployed. The authorities could not maintain their reactionary "law and order." On the eve of the 1911 Revolution the triple city of Wuhan, the crossroads of nine provinces, was smouldering with revolutionary moods, stimulated by the storm of anti-hunger movement and riots in the Yangtze River valley, and of railway agitation in neighbouring provinces. The spark of revolution was liable to flame up at any moment under the noses of the rulers in Hupeh. That the revolution broke out in Wuchang was no accident.

Besides the objective conditions, an important factor for the Wuchang Uprising was the subjective effort made by the revolutionaries, and in particular, their decade and more of effective work in units of Ching New Army stationed in Hupeh.

Wu Lu-chen, a revolutionary from Hupeh studying in Japan, had returned to Wuhan in the winter of 1902 and been appointed by Chang Chih-tung as deputy director of the department of military affairs in the province. Utilizing Chang Chih-tung's trust in him, and under cover of his legal status, he spread revolutionary ideas among the Ching troops and the educated youth. Though later transferred to Peking, he laid the ideological ground for the subsequent revolutionary movement in Hupeh.

From 1903 on, the Kuang Fu Hui (Society for the Restoration of China), the Hua Hsing Hui (Society for the Revival of the Chinese Nation) and other revolutionary organizations were set up. Influenced by revolutionary ideas, a section of the educated youth in Hupeh realized that "if you want to make revolution you must win over the ranks of the army; if you want to win over the ranks of the army you must join the army yourself." They enlisted in the New Army, distributed revolutionary magazines and books among soldiers in their units, propagated revolutionary thinking and collected forces for the revolution. In June 1904, an organization called Ko Hsueh Pu Hsi Suo (Institute for Spare-time Scientific Studies) was set up formally at Wuchang, ostensibly for the study of science, but in fact to prepare revolution. In November, it was suppressed by the Ching government, when about to respond to the Changsha Uprising led by Huang Hsing. Its principal leaders fled Wuhan, so it automatically dissolved.

In 1905, however, some of its original members exhibited revolutionary magazines and books in a reading-room in Wuchang, to attract revolutionaries. The name of this reading-room, the Jih Chih Hui (Daily Knowledge Society), was also adopted by the revolutionary organization they set up in March 1906. It expanded quickly, and at one point claimed 10,000 members. At meetings and lectures every week, they discussed the world situation, China's crisis and ways of saving the nation, influencing people from all walks of life. The Jih Chih Hui had already grown into a fairly strong revolutionary organization by August 1905, when the China Revolutionary League was founded in Japan.

Soon after establishing the League, Sun Yat-sen learned the existence and strength of this society in Wuhan. He sent men back to China for organizational contact and so gave leadership to the revolutionary activities in Hupeh.

In the winter of 1906 when the big uprisings broke out in Pinghsiang, Liuyang and Liling in Hunan Province, the Jih Chih Hui prepared to respond. But almost all its leaders, betrayed by a renegade, were arrested. So for over a year no large-scale revolutionary activities could be undertaken. However, a revolutionary organization known as the Kung Chin Hui (Society for Mutual Progress), an offshoot of the League, extended its influence to Hupeh. It became a leading centre of the revolutionary movement in the province.

In the meantime, some revolutionaries from the old Jih Chih Hui were preparing to re-establish that body. In the summer of 1908 they set up the Chun Tui Tung Meng Hui (the Army's China Revolutionary League) and, after some setbacks, resumed activity in the New Army under the names of Chun Chih Hsueh Sheh (Study Society for Democratic Government) and Chen Wu Hsueh Sheh (Study Society for Promoting Military Affairs). In 1910 Li Yuan-hung, Commander of the 21st Mixed Brigade of the Ching army in Hupeh, uncovered the revolutionary character of the Chen Wu Hsueh Sheh and launched a persecution of its leaders. But in early 1911 the revolutionaries reorganized it as the Wen Hsueh Sheh (Literary Association) and selected Chiang Yi-wu as leader to continue work. Within half a year, they had recruited over 3,000 members from the New Army.

At this juncture, there was a split in the China Revolutionary League. Sung Chiao-jen, Tan Jen-feng and some other League members from the provinces along the Yangtze disagreed with the League headquarters for concentrating its efforts too long on south China. In July 1911, they established "The Headquarters of the Central China Revolutionary League" in Shanghai. Setting up a branch in Hupeh, they took a direct part in leading the revolutionary movement there.

Deep-rooted local sectarianism had long hindered close co-operation between the two revolutionary organizations in Hupeh, the Wen Hsueh Sheh and the Kung Chin Hui. However, to meet the needs of the armed uprising, negotiations for unity were begun in the spring of 1911 with certain members of the Headquarters of the Central China Revolutionary League acting as mediators. In late September it was agreed to set up a united leading organ. Liu Kung, leader of the Kung Chin Hui, was elected *tsungli* (director-general) of the future military government. Chiang Yi-wu, leader of the Wen Hsueh Sheh, was chosen as commander-in-chief and Sun Wu, another Kung Chin Hui leader, as chief-of-staff of the uprising. Other important positions were distributed among leaders of the two organizations. The long discussions and debates brought unification, but did not resolve the contradictions. Rumour had it that Liu Kung was made *tsungli* instead of *tutuh* (military governor) to limit his power and give him no say in military affairs.

On October 8, as the uprising's chief-of-staff Sun Wu was making bombs in Hankow's Russian concession, an explosion occurred. Tsarist police rushed to the scene and seized all banners, insignia, documents and seals that had been prepared. Next day, the secret headquarters for the uprising in Wuchang was raided by the Ching gendarmes and police. Liu Yao-cheng, Peng Chu-fan and other revolutionaries were arrested; Chiang Yi-wu narrowly escaped. Other leaders fled or went into hiding. Yang Hung-sheng was seized when transporting ammunition. Some 20 other revolutionaries fell into the enemy's hands. Juicheng, Viceroy of Hupeh and Hunan, ordered the execution of all those arrested and tightly cordoned off the New Army barracks. Martial law was declared throughout Wuchang. All secret centres of the revolutionary organizations were raided. Juicheng was elated, thinking that the leading organs of the revolution had been wiped out, all revolutionaries in the New Army locked up in their barracks and the flame of the revolution extinguished. He wired the Ching government reporting "success" in nipping the revolution in the bud. But even before the Ching government had telegraphed back its commendation, the armed uprising that was to overthrow it broke out.

The time was the evening of October 10. First to rise were revolutionaries in the Eighth Engineering Battalion of the New Army. They killed the acting battalion commander, company commander and platoon leader sent to arrest them, then charged out of their barracks to seize rifles and ammunition at the Chuwangtai arsenal. Revolutionaries in its garrison threw open the gate. When the soldiers of the infantry, artillery and supplies corps and students of a military academy heard the firing, they too joined the uprising and assembled at Chuwangtai. The insurgents elected a company commander, a former member of the Jih Chih Hui (Daily Knowledge Society), as temporary commander and attacked the viceroy's yamen. Of the 22 army battalions stationed in Wuhan, five rose up, while the other 17 still obeyed their Ching commanders. The reactionary troops were more than thrice as strong as the revolutionary forces in terms of battalions. But actually the revolutionaries' underground work had won over 5,000 of the 15,000 soldiers in the Hupeh New Army — a third of all its men. Therefore the uprising paralysed the Ching command, with only a few battalions offering resistance. After stiff encounters, these were utterly routed. Juicheng and other reactionary officials, along with their families, broke through the back wall of the viceroy's yamen and fled to the gunboat *Chuyu* anchored on the Yangtze. By that night, the insurgent troops held Wuchang. On the night of the 11th and the morning of the 12th, the New Army soldiers stationed at Hankow and Hanyang joined the uprising, completely freeing the triple city of Wuhan from Ching rule. Several days later, revolutionaries launched uprisings at Yunglungho and Hanchuan, took over the counties of Tienmen, Chienli and Chienchiang — all in Hupeh — and captured over 30 vessels of the Ching government's Yangtze fleet. The situation around Wuhan was gradually stabilized. The revolution advanced with lightning speed.

The successful uprising raised the revolutionary spirit of the people in the Wuhan area. Tremendous was the rejoicing of the masses at being rid of the long dark feudal rule, and the enthusiasm with which they joined the revolution. On October 12, hearing that the revolutionary army was forming four new brigades, workers, peasants and revolutionary intellectuals flocked to enlist, making up the required number in five days. On October 16, the revolutionary army attacked Ching troops who had retreated to Liuchiamiao outside Hankow. Though without military experience, the new soldiers were brimming with revolutionary enthusiasm, and quickly captured it. Two days later they dealt head-on blows to the Ching suppression force coming down from the north. Railway workers and peasants used their tools and hoes to pursue and destroy the fleeing enemy, helping win the battle of annihilation.

The victorious Wuchang Uprising made a yawning breach in the reactionary Ching rule, and precipitated an immediate country-wide upsurge. Revolutionaries in many places rallied soldiers of the Ching New Army and members of the secret societies to join the fray. Workers, peasants and urban residents rose to reinforce the revolutionary struggle against imperialism and feudalism.

Hunan was the first other province to respond. On October 22, the revolutionaries Chiao Ta-feng and Chen Tso-hsin led insurgents in the New Army and secret societies in a drive on Changsha, killing Huang Chung-hao, the garrison commander, and driving out the provincial governor Yu Cheng-ko. Victory in Hunan removed threats to Wuchang from the rear. Shensi, Kiangsi, Shansi, Shanghai, Chekiang and Kwangtung rose up next. On November 22, revolutionaries in Chungking, Szechuan Province, led an uprising which spread over 57 sub-prefectures and counties in southeastern Szechuan. Three days later, other revolutionaries in that province, together with soldiers of the Hupeh New Army who had been sent there for suppression, revolted at Tzechow. They killed Tuanfang, who had been sent to crush the popular movement for the defence of railway rights. By then, the provinces of Yunnan, Kweichow, Kwangsi, Anhwei and Fukien had either risen in revolt or declared their independence of the Ching government. From October 10 to late November, 14 out of China's 24 provinces and regions renounced their allegiance to Ching rule.

In the provinces which had not yet declared independence, there was a rapid succession of uprisings in the New Army, stimulated by the revolutionaries, and spontaneous armed struggles of the workers and peasants. Militia units, formed by railway workers and peasants, appeared along the Peking-Hankow Railway around Hsinyang, Honan. In November, by switching or removing the tracks, they derailed or overturned trains carrying Ching troops. They also attacked grain storage depots, ammunition dumps and military supply trains, giving tremendous support to the revolutionary warfare around Wuchang. Peasant uprisings in Shantung and Liaoning had a wide impact. Even in Chihli Province, the vital centre of Ching rule, revolutionaries agitated the New Army at Luanchow and Paoting to march on Peking. Incoming reports panicked the Ching rulers.

These lightning developments mounted to the third high tide of revolution in modern Chinese history — succeeding the Taiping revolution of 1851-64 and the Yi Ho Tuan Movement of 1900-01. It swept away the reactionary Ching rule. With the Wuchang Uprising as landmark and led by the revolutionaries headed by Sun Yat-sen, it became known as the Revolution of 1911.*

---

* In Chinese, the Hsin-hai (辛亥) revolution, from the cyclic name of the lunar year here roughly corresponding to 1911.

When news of the Wuchang Uprising reached Peking, the panic-stricken Ching rulers ordered Juicheng to recapture the city at all costs, to redeem his guilt at having lost it. Simultaneously, they sent Yinchang, the Minister of War, with two corps of the Northern Army to put down the uprising — the first to be directly commanded by himself, the second by Feng Kuo-chang. The Honan army and the Yangtze fleet were likewise dispatched to Hupeh as support.

The revolutionary situation developed rapidly after Hankow and Hanyang, across the Yangtze from Wuchang, fell to the revolutionaries. Sensing the grave crisis, the handful of ruling Ching nobles found it necessary to readjust relations within the counter-revolutionary camp, to save themselves from extinction. On October 14, the regent Tsaifeng ordered the reinstatement of Yuan Shih-kai, whom he had sent home to Honan for "convalescence" three years earlier. Yuan was appointed Viceroy of Hupeh and Hunan, and ordered to Hupeh to replace Juicheng whom the revolutionary forces had driven out. Despite Yuan's three-year retirement, six divisions of the modernized Northern Army were still under the command of his henchmen Feng Kuo-chang, Wang Shih-chen and Tuan Chi-jui. It was because Yuan wielded such strength that the Ching rulers had to bow to him.

The more they relied on Yuan Shih-kai, the higher the price he demanded. Despising the viceroyalty of Hupeh and Hunan as falling short of his dignity and his counter-revolutionary ambition to dominate all China, he delayed in accepting the imperial order and remained in his home town of Changteh on the excuse that his foot "was not yet well." Secretly he directed Feng Kuo-chang's troops "to go slow and wait and see." Thus he made use of the rapidly developing revolutionary situation in the south to haggle with the Ching government. Meanwhile Yuan instructed his henchmen to demand that he be given full powers to command the army and navy and reorganize the imperial cabinet.

Yuan Shih-kai's attempt to grab all political and military power from the Ching rulers at one stroke naturally antagonized the ministers belonging to the imperial clan, leading to a deadlock.

Towards the end of October the provinces of Hunan, Shensi and Kiangsi declared their independence. Minister of War Yinchang, who had been sent to Hupeh, was unable to impose his command on the generals of the Northern Army, and suffered repeated defeats at the front. The Ching government was forced to recall Yinchang and appoint Yuan Shih-kai Imperial Envoy with full powers of command over the army and navy. This was the initial concession the Ching nobles made to Yuan.

Then a revolutionary outbreak in Shansi Province on October 29, 1911, posed a direct threat to the capital, Peking. Simultaneously, a New Army unit stationed at Luanchow (in present-day Hopei Province) issued a circular telegram demanding the convocation of a parliament and reorganization of the cabinet. It detained a trainload of arms and ammunition being transported from Russia via the Siberian railway for the suppression of the revolution in Hupeh, and declared that it would send troops to Tungchow and Nanyuan, on Peking's outskirts, to place the Ching government under military threat. The rulers were thrown into confusion by the danger under their very noses. Rather than be killed by the insurgents, they preferred to hand over the power to Yuan Shih-kai and seek his protection. On October 30 the imperial cabinet declared its own dissolution. The next day Yuan Shih-kai was appointed prime minister to organize a new one. Thus the Ching nobles finally capitulated to Yuan.

A few days earlier, Yuan had seen from the revolution's quick advance that if he remained in his home town too long the onrushing tide might sweep away Ching rule and leave him no room for counter-revolutionary manoeuvres. Hence he hurried south to direct Feng Kuo-chang in intensifying attacks on Hankow. Around that time the revolutionary forces in Wuhan appointed a reactionary army officer Chang Ching-liang as their own commander-in-chief. Chang had commanded the 29th Regiment of the Ching army in Hupeh. Pretending to support the revolution, this reactionary secretly collaborated with Yuan Shih-kai's troops, bringing repeated reverses on those of the revolution. Only when Huang Hsing arrived at Wuhan and took command was a counter-offensive launched. However, Yuan's forces were too strong and reactionaries had infiltrated the revolutionary ranks, so Huang Hsing had to withdraw to Hanyang. After occupying Hankow,

Feng Kuo-chang turned loose his soldiery to pillage, rape and set fire to innumerable dwellings which burned for three days and nights, leaving 15 kilometres of streets and markets in ruins. His vandalism infuriated the entire Chinese people.

Through the fall of Hankow, the counter-revolution again raised its head. With newly-amassed political capital, Yuan Shih-kai went to Peking to form a new cabinet on November 14. Prior to this he sent hired assassins to murder Wu Lu-chen, who had for many years been active in revolutionary work in north China. Since his transfer from Hupeh to Peking in 1903, Wu had held the posts of superintendent for military training of the Ching troops and deputy director of border affairs in Yenchi (in present-day Kirin Province), and on the eve of the Wuchang Uprising was in command of the Sixth Division of the Northern Army. He had secretly arranged with the New Army unit at Luanchow to revolt against Ching rule, and made contact with the revolutionaries in Shansi. Informed of this, Yuan Shih-kai saw Wu as a thorn in his flesh and had him assassinated. Then he stripped the principal officers of the New Army at Luanchow, who tended towards the revolution, of their command. He also broke up the attempt of Shantung Province to declare independence.

In these ways, Yuan stabilized counter-revolutionary order throughout north China. On November 19 he formed a cabinet, including his diehard followers Chao Ping-chun and Wang Shih-chen, his old-time colleague Tang Shao-yi and the constitutionalist leaders Chang Chien and Liang Chichao. Feng Kuo-chang was appointed commander of the Imperial Guards. The Guards Regiment under Yuan's personal command was moved to Peking. His counter-revolutionary clique, which had the Northern warlords as its nucleus and represented the interests of the big landlords and big bourgeoisie, took advantage of the rise of the people's revolution to seize power from the ruling Ching nobility. It became the centre of counter-revolution for the whole country. And Yuan Shih-kai rose to be head of the counter-revolutionary camp.

The important reason enabling Yuan Shih-kai to succeed the Ching regime and become political chief of the counter-revolution was that he had the support of imperialism.

As Chairman Mao says in his *On New Democracy*, **"Earlier revolutions failed in China because imperialism strangled them, and innumerable revolutionary martyrs died, bitterly lamenting the non-fulfilment of their mission."**

This was true of the Revolution of 1911. During its course the bourgeois revolutionaries nursed many illusions about imperialist sympathy and support. Yet not for a single day did the imperialists give up their attempts to strangle the Chinese revolution. From October 10, when the first shot was fired at Wuchang, they stood unhesitantly by the Ching government. The next day John Jordan, British Minister to China, reported by telegram to the London Foreign Office the news "that Wuchang was in full revolution; that the yamens had been burned; and that the viceroy, who had taken refuge on a Chinese cruiser which was anchored close to a British gunboat, ... and had asked the assistance of His Majesty's ships. . . ."[*] On October 12, Germany, too, sent three gunboats to Wuhan, and soon admitted that, on the 17th, they had been involved in the "heated battle." On October 13, the U.S. government instructed its diplomatic representatives in China, France, Germany, Italy, Britain, Japan and Russia to act promptly to gather the international reactionary forces for intervention against the Chinese revolution. Shortly afterwards the U.S. imperialists concluded an agreement with the Ching govern-

---

[*] H. F. MacNair, *Modern Chinese History Selected Readings,* Shanghai, 1927, p. 700.

ment to assist the latter's stepped-up military preparations. Other imperialist countries gave the Ching troops every facility in their attack on Hanyang, helping them to build bridges and transport troops, and supplying military intelligence and provisions.

Facts show that after the outbreak of the 1911 Revolution the imperialists, while declaring "neutrality," never stopped intervening against it and helping the Ching regime. However, they could not undertake large-scale joint armed intervention because of the international situation. It was not long before the First World War, contradictions between the imperialist countries were multiplying and the struggle for the re-division of the world was growing sharper daily. Not only in Africa but also in the Far East, the United States, Japan, Britain and Russia were contending with and checking each other.

Nevertheless, imperialism did not sit idly by. Development after the Wuchang Uprising presaged the rapid and inevitable downfall of the Ching regime. In order to speedily strangle the revolution, the imperialists, while propping up the tottering dynasty, embarked upon a new vicious plot — the fostering of another lackey, in their eyes both more "loyal" and "powerful," to be their new tool in ruling over the Chinese people. Yuan

Shih-kai, the supreme head of the Northern war-lords, was the counter-revolutionary "strong man" they quickly joined in favouring.

Yuan was an old accomplice of imperialism. He had collaborated with it in slaughtering the Chinese people during the Yi Ho Tuan Movement in 1900, winning the praise of his foreign masters. Soon after the Wuchang Uprising the imperialists began to bruit it about that "only Yuan can save the situation" and "without Yuan, everything will collapse." Only two days after it occurred, the U.S. representative in the Four-Power Consortium — of the United States, Britain, Germany and France — declared in Peking that the "rebellion" would be quelled if the Ching government could get the support of a strong man such as Yuan Shih-kai. This statement bared the imperialists' scheme. They regarded the Revolution of 1911 as a "rebellion" to be "quelled," with only a counter-revolutionary "strong man" like Yuan Shih-kai as the right lackey to do it. At a meeting of the diplomatic corps in Peking, U.S. Minister W. J. Calhoun proposed urging the Ching government to appoint Yuan Shih-kai to a key position. The majority agreed, and the U.S. minister was asked to represent them in bringing up the matter to the Ching government. The fact that the imperialists were at one in favouring Yuan naturally exerted strong pressure on the Ching court, which curried to their every whim. Yuan's appointment as Viceroy of Hupeh and Hunan came two days later.

Still unsatisfied, Yuan secretly sent underlings to the American legation in Peking to obtain a higher price. The American minister busily urged his colleagues from other countries to create public opinion for ever greater authority for Yuan. Together they criticized the Ching government for treating Yuan as just an ordinary high official, saying he should get more power. The *China Press* of Shanghai, a mouthpiece of U.S. imperialism, ran an editorial on October 15, 1911, entitled "The Men of the Hour." It openly voiced the imperialist hope in the following words: "None who watches the course of events in China can fail to notice how naturally, when a critical moment in the affairs of the Empire [the Ching regime] arrives, the name of Yuan Shih-kai rises to men's lips. The report from our Peking correspondent that the post of Generalissimo has been offered to Yuan, unfortunately carries no assurance that he will return to office at present. No position beneath an important place in the Ministry is compatible with his attainments and ability. No single act of the Government would inspire so much confidence both at home and abroad as for it to once more summon Yuan to a seat in the Councils of State."

That the high ministers of the imperial house finally handed over power to Yuan was due largely to such pressures.

When Yuan Shih-kai was made Prime Minister the imperialists exulted. In a cabled reply to John Jordan, British Minister to China, British Foreign Secretary Edward Grey said that London had most friendly feeling and respect for Yuan and would give his government all possible diplomatic support. The diplomatic corps in Peking held a meeting to congratulate Yuan. It authorized the British Minister, Jordan, to confer with him on "appropriate measures," that is, to plot to strangle the Chinese revolution, which the imperialists and Chinese big landlords and big compradores were again combining against. The counter-revolutionary political power headed by Yuan, with the Northern warlords as its nucleus, was a product of collaboration between the domestic and foreign reaction. It was an even more ferocious lackey of imperialism than those of the past.

It was by leaning on the strength of the people that the bourgeois revolutionaries had won victory over the Ching rule in the Revolution of 1911. But they were not thoroughgoing in revolution. Therefore, they quickly compromised with, and bowed to, Yuan Shih-kai's counter-revolutionary forces. The fruits of the revolution were speedily usurped by China's big landlords and big compradores.

As the foxes fled their den,
Peach-wood puppets took the stage.

This verse of Lu Hsun's graphically describes the situation in Chinese society after the Wuchang Uprising. As the Ching regime tottered towards downfall, a host of "peach-wood puppets" — ghosts and demons, big and small — came onstage to trample on the people as their predecessors had done. In north China, the counter-revolution held sway and Yuan Shih-kai's regime replaced the Ching's. In south China, controlled by revolutionary forces, numerous minor "Yuan Shih-kais" wormed their way into provincial governments and worked to usurp power. On the surface, the revolution seemed to be full of vigour. In fact it was pregnant with grave crises.

129

Prior to the Wuchang Uprising the principal leaders of the China Revolutionary League had a rather pessimistic view of the situation. They had eyes only for their own activities and those of the small number of revolutionaries. They wanted to make use of the revolutionary enthusiasm and aspirations of the workers and peasants, but were often cool and contemptuous towards them. So the repeated setbacks of the earlier uprisings caused some to desert, others to become despondent and degenerate, and still others to die in despair. Some did persist in the fight. But being isolated they could not constitute a strong leading core, still less control the course of events.

After the Wuchang Uprising the revolutionary flames generated by the army rank and file spread quickly to the whole country, powerfully impelled by the worker and peasant mass movement. The bourgeois revolutionaries made a positive contribution by starting the struggle. But the onset of the revolution itself revealed their flabbiness. As the Ching regime tottered day by day to doom, many revolutionaries gradually lost their perspective. Confronted with strong counter-revolutionary forces — Yuan Shih-kai and behind him, imperialism — even their revolutionary courage ebbed. They repeatedly pledged themselves to protect imperialist privileges in China. And by brandishing the big stick of "orderly revolution" they schemed to gain the sympathy of imperialism and the feudal warlords in exchange for their own despicable manoeuvres to suppress the masses and preserve the semi-colonial and semi-feudal social order. More and more, they interpreted revolution purely as the overthrow of the Ching government. So they declared that anyone who opposed the Ching Dynasty and supported the republic could be considered a comrade, thinking that this could win over Yuan Shih-kai and the Ching officials at different levels.

But things turned out just the opposite. Their compromising with imperialism and the feudal forces was utilized by counter-revolutionary elements to wriggle into the revolutionary ranks, pilfer the fruits of revolution from within, and hand them over to Yuan Shih-kai. This happened in different provinces after the Wuchang Uprising. One by one they declared independence, and one by one the local organs of power at every level fell into the hands of reaction, though this process took different forms.

The first form was represented by Hupeh, the "seat of the uprising," taking shape in places where the revolutionaries had kindled uprisings by the New Army and the secret societies. For lack of strong leadership, the political and military power there quickly reverted to the grasp of old officials, constitutionalists and other reactionaries. From the very beginning, the sword was in hands other than those of the revolutionaries.

In Wuchang on the morning of October 11, after the previous night's intense fighting, the revolutionary soldiers gathered at the Hupeh provincial consultative assembly building to set up revolutionary power and elect a provincial military governor. Many people there were influenced by the theory that "certain people are the first to know and become aware" and the idealistic view that "history is made by heroes," spread by the bourgeois revolutionaries. So they thought the rank-and-file soldiers who had taken part in the uprising could not produce anyone qualified to be military governor, and while some were nominated for the post none were accepted. As for the leaders of the Wen Hsueh Sheh (Literary Association) and the Kung Chin Hui (Society for Mutual Progress) who had organized the uprising, some had been arrested and killed, others compelled to flee for their lives on its eve. So nobody of influence was left to be elected. The constitutionalists, who had wormed their way into this meeting, seized the chance to propose Li Yuan-hung as military governor.

Li Yuan-hung, born in Huangpi County, Hupeh, a graduate of the Northern Naval College, had served in the Northern Fleet. Becoming a follower of Chang Chih-tung, Viceroy of Hupeh and Hunan, he was appointed to command a cavalry battalion in the Ching army. Promoted to head the 21st Mixed Brigade, he became the most effective accomplice of Chang Chih-tung and other power-holders in Hupeh. On the night of October 10, at his post in the army barracks, he shot and killed by his own hand a soldier who favoured the uprising. Later he killed a liaison man the revolutionaries sent to contact him. Only upon hearing that the viceroy Juicheng had fled and the revolutionaries held Wuchang did he hurriedly hide out in a staff officer's house. At ordinary times, Li affected a hypocritical air of generosity and broad-mindedness, which deceived many. Moreover, the China Revolutionary League itself, in its "Programme for Revolution" and other documents, had spread illusions about the Han landlords and officials, leading some people to think that Li with his "high prestige" would "have a broad appeal" if elected head of the Hupeh military government. So, as soon as his name was brought up the great majority of the revolutionaries approved. Li himself, however, did not accept immediately, as he was not sure the Ching rule would really be overthrown. He took the post only when the revolutionaries forced him to, at pistol point, and even then did not utter a word and stubbornly refused to cut off his queue, the badge of loyalty to the Ching Dynasty. The revolutionaries proceeded to organize a "strategy department" to exercise military command. But they did not pay much attention to administrative and diplomatic matters. Consequently, Tang Hua-lung, a leader of the constitutionalists and speaker of the Hupeh Provincial Consultative Assembly, was chosen to head the department of civil affairs. Tang swore in words to "devote his life to duty," but at the same time secretly telegraphed the Ching government that he would "never join the rebels." Thus, from the very birth of the new Hupeh military government, reactionaries usurped both its military and civil administration.

With the later development of the revolution, these reactionary elements, who had penetrated into its organs of power, realized that the Ching regime could not last long. So they became all the more active in grabbing more authority and disintegrating the revolution from within. The crafty Tang Hua-lung began to woo certain waverers among the members of the China Revolutionary League headquarters who had arrived at Wuhan. At a conference on October 16 he proposed the adoption of "Provisional Regulations of the Organization of the Military Governor's Office," which he claimed had been drafted by the League headquarters. These regulations, which were promulgated, abolished the "strategy department" and thus deprived the revolutionaries of power in military matters. The military governor, Li Yuan-hung, became concurrently commander-in-chief of the revolutionary army. Then he changed the "department of civil affairs" into the "department of political affairs" with himself wielding the real executive authority, while Tang Hua-lung remained as its head. With this, Li Yuan-hung assumed power, issuing orders and directives.

Furthermore, the reactionaries took advantage of the disunity between revolutionaries belonging respectively to the Wen Hsueh Sheh and the Kung Chin Hui to sow more dissension among them, instigating them to mutual attacks and betrayals to undermine the revolutionary forces. Reaction grew so strong as the revolution weakened in Hupeh that Huang Hsing, after arriving in Wuhan, was compelled to play second fiddle to Li Yuan-hung. In the first revolutionary government, the position of a leader of the bourgeois revolutionary party was not even up to that of a counter-revolutionary butcher like Li Yuan-hung. The rest can easily be imagined.

Similar situations arose, after the Wuchang Uprising, in Shensi, Chekiang, Fukien and some other provinces.

The second form was represented by Hunan where the revolutionaries had aroused the New Army and secret societies to revolt and overthrow the old rule in fierce battles. Chiao Ta-feng and Chen Tso-hsin, both revolutionaries, became military governor and deputy military governor. But again, the revolutionaries lacked vigilance, and did not wage a thorough fight against the reactionary forces. Instead of completely breaking up the old Hunan military formations, they took them over intact. This enabled the reactionaries, specifically the constitutionalists, to buy over some officers of similar views to theirs in the New Army. These incited the soldiers to rebel and kill Chiao Ta-feng and Chen Tso-hsin. Tan Yen-kai, a leader of the constitutionalists, seized the chance to install himself as military governor of Hunan.

A similar usurpation of power occurred in Kweichow. After the victory of the revolution in Kweiyang, capital of that province, on November 4, disputes arose between two factions in the revolutionary camp. One wanted to suppress the reactionaries. The other urged "generosity to avoid enmity." The latter won out, and it was decided to give the revolutionaries and constitutionalists an equal number of posts in the new revolutionary government. The revolutionaries thus went the wrong way at their very first step.

Before the Kweiyang uprising the Ching governor there had telegraphically summoned an army unit to nip it in the bud. The uprising succeeded while it was still on the way, leaving it up in the air. Arguments arose among the revolutionaries: some suggested liquidating this reactionary force to save future trouble; others said it could be utilized, and that it would not be too late to deal with it should it not submit to orders. The latter view prevailed. The revolutionaries let these troops enter Kweiyang intact for incorporation, and supplied them with plenty of arms and ammunition. Later, the constitutionalists used this same force to rebel, and to kill many revolutionaries. Also, they colluded with the Yunnan warlord Tang Chi-yao in wiping out nearly all of Kweichow's chief revolutionary leaders. These bourgeois revolutionaries, having taken pity on snake-like scoundrels, died at their hands. It was a historical lesson.

Of *the third form*, Kiangsu Province was an example. The success of an uprising by Shanghai revolutionaries on November 3 stimulated the vigorous development of the mass movement and risings of the New Army in many places. Under the compelling impetus of the revolution, the constitutionalists and the upper sections of the gentry-merchants of Soochow (then the provincial capital) urged Kiangsu's governor, Cheng Teh-chuan, to declare the province independent to forestall attacks by the revolutionary forces. Cheng agreed, and on November 5 simply renamed his governor's yamen the "Office of the Military Governor for Kiangsu Province of the Military Government of the Republic of China," and himself "military governor." He held a ceremony and made a hypocritical speech, after which a revolutionary sent from Shanghai handed him his new seal of office. This was called the victory of the revolution in Kiangsu. A news report commented: "Soochow has been 'recovered' without the slightest change except for a few tiles on the roof of the governor's yamen which were lifted off with a bamboo pole to show that a revolution must involve destruction." This stinging remark struck like a whip-lash at the lack of thoroughness of the bourgeois revolution.

Two days later the governor of Kwangsi Province, Shen Ping-kun, proclaimed its independence in the same manner. Having got news of such declarations by several provinces, he realized which way the wind was blowing. On November 6 he called his subordinates to a meeting which decided to put on a show by ordering hundreds of big-character posters to be written overnight and plastered in the streets of Kweilin, the provincial capital. They read: "The National Army of the entire Great Han Province of Kwangsi respectfully requests Governor Shen to declare independence. Long live the future of Kwangsi!" On the morning of November 7 the constitutionalists met in the provincial consultative assembly house and elected Shen military governor. Kwangsi simplified even the Kiangsu pattern. However, Shen Ping-kun remained in his new post for only a few days. Then Lu Jung-ting, hitherto the Ching army's provincial commander-in-chief, staged an armed revolt and seized military and political power from him.

In some other provinces the situation was complicated, with various twists and turns. Power appeared to be in the hands of the revolutionaries, but some soon swerved to the Right, others turned into reactionary politicians, and still others into provincial warlords. Their rule was no better than the old government's. This applied, in general, to provinces like Kwangtung, Szechuan and Anhwei.

After provincial independence, the power in some was held by the bourgeois revolutionaries, in others old officials who had wormed their way into the revolutionary ranks. But one characteristic was common to both: the mass movements of the workers and peasants were suppressed and the masses disarmed. In independent Kwangtung, the revolutionaries themselves admitted, while 90,000 militia members were disbanded in the provincial capital alone, counter-revolutionary troops under the Ching commander Lung Chi-kuang were left intact. In Szechuan, the Army of Comrades for Railway Protection, numbering hundreds of thousands, was disbanded and some of its fighters killed as "bandits of the secret societies." Where old officials held the power, some of the reactionary troops were simply renamed the "National Army," others, already routed by revolutionary troops, were regrouped as soon as reaction got back the upper hand. By contrast, mass movements of the workers and peasants and of the lower ranks of the revolutionary forces were invariably banned. From the very start, the new-born bourgeois-revolutionary power took its stand against the masses. The radical bourgeois revolutionaries were quick to flare up, but even quicker to retreat. They could never lead the people to real victory. It was owing to these objectively determined circumstances that Sun Yat-sen made concessions at every step in his subsequent struggle against Yuan Shih-kai.

The internal crisis of the revolution was apparent not only from the immediate usurpation of power by reactionary officials and constitutionalists in the provinces declaring independence. Even more significantly, it showed itself in the rapid disintegration of the China Revolutionary League.

The spread of the provincial independence movement between the Wuchang Uprising and late November 1911 necessitated the establishment of unified, nation-wide revolutionary state power. But how was it to be set up, and who would wield it? On this fundamental question in revolution, the lack of thoroughness of the bourgeois revolution was again revealed. In pursuit of power for some clique or individual, quite a few of its protagonists did not hesitate to collude with reactionary forces. Divisions and realignments occurred on a large scale among the revolutionaries, the constitutionalists and the old officials. Small factions and groups scrambling for power appeared in Shanghai and Wuchang. As a result the China Revolutionary League, once a standard for bourgeois-democratic revolution, broke up. The small factions and groups gradually coalesced into two centres — the Min Sheh (People's Society) in Wuchang and the Kung Ho Tung Yi Hui (United Republican Society) in Shanghai. The bourgeois revolutionary Chang Tai-yen said after the Wuchang Uprising, "The revolutionary army is rising, the revolutionary party is disappearing." He himself was one of the leading splitters, and his words described the actual state of affairs.

The Min Sheh, whose core was a group of Hupeh careerists, aimed at maintaining the political status of that provincial clique. Li Yuan-hung was its leader, and the principal members included a number of his henchmen, some members of the China Revolutionary League from Hupeh such as Lan Tien-wei and Sun Wu, and Tan Yen-kai, leader of the constitutionalists in Hunan. They published a newspaper and declared their "progressivism," but with the real aim of opposing Sun Yat-sen and overthrowing Huang Hsing. Making use of the political position assumed by Wuchang, where the uprising had begun, they prepared to make it the national capital to grab control of the central power.

The Kung Ho Tung Yi Hui was a clique comprising many politicians clustering in Shanghai. It was founded by Chen Chi-mei, the city's military governor, Wu Ting-fang, a member of the China Revolutionary League, Chang Chien, a leading constitutionalist, and Wang Ching-wei, the traitor bought over by Yuan Shih-kai. They collaborated with constitutionalist leaders from Kiangsu and Chekiang and reactionary officials like Cheng Teh-chuan and Tang Shou-chien, likewise with the aim of organizing and controlling the central power. They thought they could rely on the authoritative position of these men as their main force in gaining control.

Amid intense activity by these old and new politicians, movements to organize a central government began simultaneously in Wuchang and Shanghai, accompanied by a struggle for leadership between the two cliques.

On November 9 the Wuchang group, in the name of Li Yuan-hung, asked the provinces which had declared independence to make nominations by telegraph for ministerial posts; those gaining the most votes were to be sent to Wuchang to organize the provisional central government. This group held that the Wuchang government should

143

be that of the whole country, and be legitimized as such as soon as the provinces approved its list of ministers and foreign countries recognized it. On November 11 the Shanghai group likewise wired the provinces to send representatives to attend a provisional conference — but in Shanghai. Four days later, it was held there, under the name of "Joint Conference of the Representatives of the Provincial Military Governors' Offices." Shanghai thus seized priority in organization.

From November 17 to 20 the Shanghai conference discussed Li Yuan-hung's circular to the provinces. On the grounds of the city's easy communications it decided that the joint conference should be held there, and asked Wuchang to send representatives. At the same time it recognized the Wuchang Military Government as the Central Military Government and the exercise of central administrative power by the military governor of Hupeh. It asked Wuchang, acting as the central government, to appoint Wu Ting-fang and Wen Tsung-yao, both of whom had been elected by the provincial representatives, as the central government's diplomatic representatives. Li Yuan-hung, greatly displeased, sent an envoy to Shanghai to raise objections. So the Shanghai group had to change its decision. The new arrangement was for each province to keep a liaison man in Shanghai while the actual question of organizing the provisional central government was left over for discussion in Wuchang.

At the end of November, the provincial representatives arrived at Wuchang from Shanghai. Just then the Hunan-Hupeh Joint Army under the command of Huang Hsing was sustaining heavy defeats at the hands of counter-attacking Ching troops. Hanyang was lost, and Wuchang threatened with enemy bombardment. Hence, the representatives had to meet in the British concession at Hankow. The meeting lasted three days. In the meantime, the Kiangsu-Chekiang Joint Army, formed by the Shanghai group in late November, had captured Nanking. It was then decided that Nanking should be the seat of the provisional government, the representatives were to proceed there within a week to continue the conference, and that as soon as those from more than 10 provinces came, they would elect the provisional president.

The loss of Hanyang and capture of Nanking changed the relative positions of the Wuchang and Shanghai groups. The former were weakened, the latter strengthened. Seizing their chance, Chen Chi-mei, Military Governor of Shanghai, and other bourgeois politicians, acting jointly with Cheng Teh-chuan and Tang Shou-chien, invited the provincial liaison representatives who had remained in Shanghai to meet on December 4. They claimed that with Hanyang lost and Wuchang in danger, the representatives conference at Hankow could no longer organize a provisional government. Hence they decided to make Nanking its seat, and elect Huang Hsing as Generalissimo to preside over its formation, with Li Yuan-hung as deputy. This enraged the Wuhan group. In Li Yuan-hung's name, it immediately telegraphed objections to the military governors of the provinces.

While the politicians of Shanghai and Wuchang were contesting for leadership in forming the provisional government, Yuan Shih-kai's representative for "peace negotiations," Tang Shao-yi, arrived at Hankow with British, U.S. and other imperialists pulling the strings from behind the scenes. This further complicated the struggle.

The "peace" offensive and military pressure were the counter-revolutionary dual tactics alternately used by Yuan Shih-kai. In late October when he went south personally to direct the attack on Hankow, Yuan had ordered his henchman Liu Cheng-en, who hailed from the same county as Li Yuan-hung, to write to the latter expressing Yuan's desire for peace and promising that if Li and the others laid down their arms, the past would be forgotten and they would receive high posts. After occupying Hankow, Yuan followed with another peace feeler. The Wuchang group replied that if only Yuan did not oppose the Han people's revolution they would elect him president. Soon, Yuan Shih-kai sent a representative to Wuchang to talk with Li and his group. But Huang Hsing and other revolutionaries firmly opposed this "peace." It was because Yuan failed to achieve his counter-revolutionary objective that he ordered a heavy attack on Hanyang.

After occupying Hanyang on November 27, the Ching troops commanded by Yuan bombarded Wuchang from the Tortoise Hill across the river. Huang Hsing beat a retreat. Claiming repeatedly that the enemy's gunfire was too fierce to withstand, he suggested abandoning Wuchang and turning to attack Nanking. Drawing a reprimand by the Wuchang political clique, he left for Shanghai the same afternoon. Then, on December 1 the military governor's office in Wuchang was hit and set on fire by an enemy shell. Li Yuan-hung, scared out of his wits, fled to nearby Kotien with two platoons of bodyguards, and Wuchang was thrown into confusion. The crafty Yuan Shih-kai kept on bombarding it but did not order a crossing of the river. He made use of the siege to force Wuchang into more concessions. Such was the situation when Yuan's "peace" representative came to Hankow.

On December 10 the provincial representatives who had originally met in both Shanghai and Hankow streamed into Nanking, making ready to choose a president. Before they assembled, word came that Yuan's representative was in Hankow. This made them waver in introducing the resolution for electing a president. The Wuchang politicians, who earlier had objected to Shanghai's decision, now thought the presidency should be reserved for Yuan Shih-kai. Making a turnabout, they agreed with the Shanghai side to make Huang Hsing Generalissimo with the function of temporary president. But no sooner was this compromise reached than the Kiangsu-Chekiang Joint Army declared that they would not serve under a defeated general like Huang Hsing and preferred Li Yuan-hung as Generalissimo. Hence the representatives once more named Li with Huang Hsing as deputy. Huang, however, refused to accept this secondary position. Things dragged and in late December the provisional government had still not been formed.

The site of the peace negotiations was another key issue in the fight for leadership. After Yuan's peace negotiator arrived at Hankow, the Shanghai side raised strong objections to conferring there, notifying Yuan that they would not recognize any agreement between him and Wuchang. Yuan himself had considered Li Yuan-hung the best person to parley with, because the latter was not a revolutionary and was liable to compromise under threat of bombardment from Hanyang. But the Shanghai side persisted in its demand. Yuan then reckoned that since foreign imperialist influence was stronger in Shanghai than in Hankow, negotiations there might be more to his advantage. He therefore agreed to Shanghai's proposal. On December 17 Tang Shao-yi arrived in that city.

The next day the first meeting took place between Tang Shao-yi and Wu Ting-fang, representing the revolutionary army. Cease-fire agreements were concluded for Hupeh, Shensi, Shansi, Anhwei, Kiangsu and Fengtien (now Liaoning) provinces. Then the British consul at Shanghai, together with those of the U.S., Japan, Russia, Germany and France, called on the negotiating representatives to advise the two sides to quickly reach an accord and stop hostilities. Though feigning impartiality, these imperialists were actually exerting pressure on the south to stop revolutionary action and surrender to Yuan Shih-kai. At the second meeting, on December 20, Wu Ting-fang declared that the negotiations must be premised on the recognition of a republican form of government. But at the same time he tipped off Tang Shao-yi that the south would be ready to reward Yuan Shih-kai with the presidency if he forced the Ching emperor to abdicate. Tang's task had been to negotiate southern recognition of Yuan's position. Attaining his objective, he declared equivocally that the question of monarchy or democracy should be reserved for discussion and decision by parliament when it was convoked.

On December 25, a few days after the compromise between Wu Ting-fang and Tang Shao-yi, Sun Yat-sen returned from abroad, bringing hope and courage to the radical revolutionaries. They campaigned for Sun's election as president, but indicated that he would be asked to concede the post to Yuan if the latter "came over." The election was held on December 29. Representatives from 17 provinces took part, each with one vote, and Sun received 16 votes. On New Year's Day of 1912, Sun Yat-sen took the presidential oath, and declared the founding of the Republic of China. On January 3 the provincial representatives elected Li Yuan-hung vice-president, passed the list of nine cabinet members proposed by Sun, and set up the provisional government of the republic. At the end of the month the senate was formed. Despite the fact that the Nanking provisional government included constitutionalists and old officials, the revolutionaries still held the leadership of the state power. They embarked on the establishment of a bourgeois-democratic republic and within a short period proclaimed a number of policies and decrees compatible with the revolution's interests. In the minds of the people, therefore, the founding of the republic was a death sentence to the reactionary Ching rule.

With Sun Yat-sen as leader the revolutionaries used the Nanking provisional government as a weapon against Yuan Shih-kai. Sun telegraphed Yuan expressing readiness to give up the presidency in his favour if Yuan supported the republic. At the same time, through Wu Ting-fang, conditions were presented to Yuan, who was told he would be received at Nanking and made president as soon as the republic was securely established.

Yuan Shih-kai's counter-revolutionary clique, backed by imperialism, responded with an immediate counter-attack. On the day Sun Yat-sen was sworn in as president, Yuan told a henchman to secretly wire Tang Shao-yi to resign as peace negotiator, and the Northern warlord Tuan Chi-jui, commander of the First Army, issued a circular telegram swearing to "struggle to the death if the republican form is adopted by minority opinion." The next day Yuan wired Wu Ting-fang that Tang Shao-yi had exceeded his authority, so all the terms he had negotiated with the south were void. Yuan's blackmailing threat of military force was supported by the imperialist powers. They declared they would recognize the republic only when Yuan had unified the north and south. Thus they tried to compel Sun Yat-sen to give up the presidency. Moreover, they exerted pressure, both military and economic, on the Nanking government.

The constitutionalists and old officials who had wormed their way into the Nanking provisional government worked hand in glove with Yuan's counter-revolutionary clique in this counter-attack. With their subsidiary factions and organizations, they burrowed like termites to wreck the revolutionary ranks from within. They raised an open demand for the dissolution of the China Revolutionary League led by Sun Yat-sen, whom they criticized as being "too idealistic" and "hankering after position and wealth." Persons like Wang Ching-wei even charged that Sun's unwillingness to compromise with Yuan stemmed from reluctance to part with the presidential office. All along, they hoped that the fighting would stop so that Yuan Shih-kai would unify the north and south and they themselves find positions in his government. Through the efforts of these political hucksters, secret backstage bargaining was stepped up behind the apparent standstill in negotiations. The bargaining centred around one proposition: Yuan Shih-kai was to force the Ching emperor to abdicate as a price for his own accession to the presidency.

Under such pressure by both domestic and foreign counter-revolutionary forces, the revolutionaries headed by Sun Yat-sen began to compromise. On January 22, 1912, Sun directed Wu Ting-fang to inform Yuan that, as soon as the south received authentic news of the Ching emperor's abdication and Yuan's public declaration of support for the republic, he would resign and the senate would choose Yuan Shih-kai president. Yuan, satisfied, set out to force the emperor to step down. On January 26, the warlords headed by Tuan Chi-jui, who had previously circulated a telegram against a republic, sent another to the Ching government, signed with more than 40 names, demanding that a republic be set up. The handful of the Ching nobles and ministers had no alternative but to accept the conditions, including "favourable treatment of the imperial family," proposed by the revolutionaries. On February 12, the emperor Puyi (Hsuan Tung) issued his abdication edict. On the following day Yuan Shih-kai wired the Nanking provisional government demanding the presidency. On the 14th Sun Yat-sen resigned, and the next day the Nanking senate elected Yuan Shih-kai president. Each of the 17 provinces had one vote and all 17 were cast for Yuan, one vote more than when it had elected Sun Yat-sen.

Although forced to resign, Sun Yat-sen hoped to preserve the bourgeois-democratic republic founded in the revolution. His resignation message to the senate included three proposals:

1.   The provisional government should be set up in Nanking;

2.   The president and cabinet members should resign only when the new president elected by the senate arrived at Nanking and took office;

3.   The new president must observe the provisional constitution of the provisional government whose decrees and regulations were to remain in force unless revised by the senate.

Sun Yat-sen's intention was clearly to get Yuan Shih-kai to leave Peking, the old base where feudal forces were entrenched, and serve as president in the south where the revolutionary forces were strong. He also wanted to restrain Yuan through the provisional constitution, preventing him from becoming dictator.

Towards the end of February 1912, Nanking sent Tsai Yuan-pei and others as envoys to Peking to welcome Yuan to the south. Yuan received them with a show of great enthusiasm, saying that he was "perfectly willing to go south at an early date," and travel to Wuhan first to call on Li Yuan-hung prior to taking office in Nanking. His honeyed words dispelled all the envoys' doubts. Meanwhile Yuan was laying his plot. On the evening of February 29 at the height of drinking and merriment at a sumptuous feast he was giving for the southern envoys, an artillery shell roared over the hall followed by the crack of rifle shots and flashes in the sky. It was a "mutiny" by the Third Division of the Northern Army which had started to loot and burn. The house where the envoys were staying was broken into and their retinue, not attending the reception, had to seek refuge in a foreign church. The next day more "mutinies" broke out, in Paoting, Tientsin and elsewhere. Colluding with Yuan in his plot the imperialist diplomatic corps in Peking decided to send troops to invade the capital for its "protection." Japan was the first to bring garrison units from Shanhaikuan and south Manchuria, landing at

Chinwangtao and pushing on towards Peking. The situation took a sharp critical turn. It seemed as though the invasion of the eight-power allied army in 1900 was about to be re-enacted.

The "mutinies" in Peking and elsewhere frightened the southern envoys into quickly forgetting their mission. Instead they asked that the provisional government be set up in Peking. The reactionary forces within the revolutionary camp itself seized on a new pretext. They accused the revolutionaries of being heedless of the nation's security and causing a crisis in the north by being too stubborn. Li Yuan-hung went so far as to issue a circular telegram which said, "Giving up Nanking will not cause disturbance, but giving up Peking will invite disaster," — echoing the tunes of the Yuan Shih-kai counter-revolutionary clique. Simultaneously Yuan's own henchman, Tuan Chi-jui, and other warlords clamoured in another circular telegram: "The provisional government must be established in Peking and the president, in taking office, must not leave Peking even temporarily."

Besieged by domestic and foreign counter-revolutionary forces, the already isolated bourgeois revolutionaries headed by Sun Yat-sen fell into even greater helplessness. They had to bow to a resolution of the Nanking senate, engineered by the constitutionalists, providing that the provisional government be set up in Peking. On March 10 Yuan Shih-kai took office in Peking as provisional president. On March 23 the Nanking senate, at Yuan's recommendation, approved the appointment of Tang Shao-yi as premier. On April 1 Sun Yat-sen announced his resignation as provisional president, and on April 5 the senate resolved to move the provisional government to Peking. By then the bourgeois and petty-bourgeois revolutionaries had dismantled their last line of defence. The big landlords and big compradores, supported by imperialism, officially usurped the fruits of the victory of the people's revolution and set up the counter-revolutionary dictatorship headed by Yuan Shih-kai. The history of the Revolution of 1911 came to a virtual end.

The Chinese people's great leader Chairman Mao Tsetung has concisely and scientifically summed up the Revolution of 1911: **"The revolution started by Dr. Sun Yat-sen has had both its successes and its failures. Was not the Revolution of 1911 a success? Didn't it send the emperor packing? Yet it was a failure in the sense that while it sent the emperor packing it left China under imperialist and feudal oppression, so that the anti-imperialist and anti-feudal revolutionary task remained unaccomplished."**

China's society had been feudal. After the Opium War of 1840, it was transformed, step by step, into a semi-colonial and semi-feudal one. The feudal monarchy had wielded supreme authority. The Revolution of 1911 toppled this idol, overthrew Ching Dynasty rule, and put an end to the 2,000-year-old feudal absolute monarchy. This was a new great beginning in modern Chinese history. After it the imperialists and domestic reactionaries still collaborated in repeated attempts to restore the feudal monarchy in China. But all their idiotic counter-revolutionary schemes to reverse the flow of history met with ignominious defeat. Yuan Shih-kai made himself emperor in 1915, but only for 83 days after which his "reign of Hung Hsien" was thrown on the refuse heap of history. The monarchical restoration in 1917 by the warlord Chang Hsun, who re-installed the abdicated Ching emperor, lasted but 11 days. These were obvious signs. Sun Yat-sen issued the call: "Let all the people of the country attack anyone who dares make himself emperor!" If it can be said that the historical tragedy of the bourgeois reformists was that they clung to and worshipped the emperor in the vain hope of performing a miracle, then it must be said the most significant result of the revolution achieved by the bourgeois revolutionaries led by Sun Yat-sen was to send the emperor packing and put an end to 2,000 years of feudal monarchy in China.

Nevertheless, the nature of things is determined not by name but by essence, not by form but by content. Modern history has shown that whether a state adopts a monarchical or a democratic-republican form of government is not the key issue. The main thing is which class holds power, whose class interests its policies represent. After the Revolution of 1911 the "republic" dreamed of by the bourgeois revolutionaries was formally set up, but this did not in the least change the character of China's semi-colonial and semi-feudal society. From the arch-traitor Yuan Shih-kai to the autocrat and traitor to the people Chiang Kai-shek, they and their ilk, large and small, all used the "republic" to cloak the counter-revolutionary character of their warlord and big bourgeois-fascist dictatorship. The signboard "Republic of China" hoisted by the Revolution of 1911 hung over the gate of all the traitor governments. This is clear proof that a mere change of name is unimportant. What must change is the content.

The issue of the relation between content and form, between essence and name applies to the relationship between the state system and the system of government. By the state system we mean the position of the different social classes in the state. By the system of government we mean the form of the governing structure. The Revolution of 1911 merely sent the emperor packing without altering the position of different social classes in the state. As China remained under imperialist and feudal oppression, the character of the society did not change, nor did the content of the counter-revolutionary dictatorship. Thus, the bourgeois-led revolution failed in the end. The failure can be summed up in one sentence: The Chinese bourgeoisie had neither the ability nor the means to lead the vast and difficult task of completing the anti-imperialist and anti-feudal democratic revolution.

The Revolution of 1911 belonged to the old world revolution, that is, the world bourgeois revolution. Its formula for a republic was learned from the Western bourgeoisie, from the French Republic and the American War of Independence. But by then the world bourgeois revolution already belonged to the past, and Western capitalism itself had entered the stage of monopolistic imperialism. Imperialism was tightening its rule over the colonies and semi-colonies, either in direct form or indirectly by fostering the feudal forces in those countries. Therefore, if semi-colonial and semi-feudal China wanted to win victory in her democratic revolution, a thoroughgoing anti-imperialist and anti-feudal programme was essential. China's bourgeois revolutionaries, however, had no such programme. They harboured grave illusions about imperialism and had close links with the feudal forces. These causes determined their lack of a resolute revolutionary line and their attitudes of compromise, capitulationism and defeatism in the struggles against imperialism and feudalism.

In an anti-imperialist and anti-feudal democratic revolution, the masses in their millions must be aroused to join the fight. The bourgeois revolutionaries of 1911 did make use of the fighting strength of the masses, but it was impossible for them to have a real revolutionary line of relying on and organizing the masses. Instead they feared the masses, and placed them under many restraints. No sooner had the Wuchang Uprising won initial victory, and many provinces followed suit, than they set up as "rulers" repressing the workers and peasants and disarming the masses. Many people were shot on charges of "posing as revolutionaries" or "overstepping the limits." Inevitably, by such actions, the revolutionaries lost popular support. When the domestic and foreign reactionary forces counter-attacked, they were in disarray and no longer able to fight back.

The failure of the 1911 Revolution taught the Chinese people a profound historical lesson. They learned that imperialism is their most ferocious enemy, and that they should entertain no illusions whatsoever about imperialism but on the contrary wage a most resolute and thorough struggle against it. They learned that if China wanted independence, if the Chinese nation wanted liberation, it was imperative to drive the imperialist aggressors out of the country and to destroy the feudal-compradore forces, the base of imperialist rule within the country. This great revolutionary objective could be achieved only through hard struggles by China's hundreds of millions of people under the leadership of her working class and its vanguard, the Chinese Communist Party. So after the Revolution of 1911, amid many twists and turns, the glorious task of fighting imperialism and feudalism was placed by history on the shoulders of the Chinese working class.

In "On the People's Democratic Dictatorship" Chairman Mao points out: **"The entire history of revolution proves that without the leadership of the working class revolution fails and that with the leadership of the working class revolution triumphs. In the epoch of imperialism, in no country can any other class lead any genuine revolution to victory. This is clearly proved by the fact that the many revolutions led by China's petty**

bourgeoisie and national bourgeoisie all failed."
Chairman Mao's teaching defines the direction of
advance in China's modern history.

Index

辛 亥 革 命

《中国近代史丛书》编写组

*

外文出版社出版（北京）

1976年（32开）第一版

编号：（英）11050—88

00080

11—E—1373P